Writers on Writing

EDITED BY JAMES ROBERTS, BARRY MITCHELL,
ROGER ZUBRINICH

Penguin Books

Penguin Books

Published by the Penguin Group
Penguin Books Australia Ltd
250 Camberwell Road,
Camberwell, Victoria 3124, Australia
Penguin Books Ltd
80 Strand, London WC2R 0RL, England
Penguin Putnam Inc.
375 Hudson Street, New York, New York 10014, USA
Penguin Books Canada Limited
10 Alcorn Avenue, Toronto, Ontario, Canada M4V 3B2
Penguin Books (NZ) Ltd
Cnr Rosedale and Airborne Roads, Albany, Auckland, New Zealand
Penguin Books (South Africa) (Pty) Ltd
24 Sturdee Avenue, Rosebank, Johannesburg 2196, South Africa
Penguin Books India (P) Ltd
11, Community Centre, Panchsheel Park, New Delhi 110 017, India

First published by Penguin Books Australia 2002

10 9 8 7 6 5 4 3 2

Designed by Marina Messiha, Penguin Design Studio
Cover photography by Getty Images
Typeset in 10.5/15.5 pt Legacy Serif Book by Post Pre-press Group, Brisbane, Queensland
Printed and bound in Australia by McPherson's Printing Group, Maryborough, Victoria

National Library of Australia
Cataloguing-in-Publication data:

Writers on writing: top Australian and international authors talk about their work.

ISBN 0 14 026728 X.

1. Fiction – Authorship. 2. Fiction – Technique. 3.
Authors – Interviews. 4. Authors, Australian – Interviews.
I. Zubrinich, Roger. II. Roberts, James, 1954– . III. Mitchell, Barry, 1951– .

808.3

Assisted by the Government of South Australia through Arts South Australia

Government
of South Australia   A R T S A

www.penguin.com.au

Penguin Books

Writers on Writing

James Roberts is a freelance writer and director who has worked on documentaries, educational series and multi-media projects; he has also worked as a film editor. Barry Mitchell is currently the executive producer of lifelong learning series for ABC television and has previously produced, directed and written short films and documentaries. Roger Zubrinich is the co-ordinator of AIT Arts–Professional Writing at the Adelaide Institute of Technical and Further Education. All three were involved in the production of the ABC series *Writers on Writing*, originally developed as a television program, then as a radio program, and which forms the basis of this book.

contents

introduction

Vikram Seth was fascinated by the huntsman spider crawling behind the faded portrait of the Queen. Thomas Keneally patrolled the cases of military trophies, recalling the names of historic battles. Richard Ford recognised Vietnam War memorabilia and acknowledged the reputation of Australian soldiers.

It was an anachronistic setting for interviewing writers – the Officers' Mess of the Adelaide Universities Regiment of the Australian Army Reserve – but it was the closest suitable location to the Writers' Week tents of the 2000 Adelaide Festival of Arts. We needed a quiet place to interview writers for an ABC project called *Writers on Writing*, which became a television series, a radio series, a web site and, now, a book.

We asked the writers about their working methods. What was it like to face a blank page every day, to get a rejection letter, to find an agent, to rewrite a whole book from third person to first person narration? How did they plot a story, do research and develop characters? Why did they use index cards, trust their editors, read aloud and cut adverbs? When did they begin writing, start revising and seek feedback?

What emerged was a cornucopia of insight into the working life of an eclectic group of writers. They were Indian, Canadian, Irish, English, Scottish, American and Australian. Their works ranged from plays and poetry to novels and biography. There were fifty years between the oldest and youngest, and in literary style they encompassed every variation.

Fay Weldon borrowed the sound recordist's glasses to read from her book and absent-mindedly left them on for the start of her interview. Luke Davies generously offered a choice of shirts to complement the background curtains. Jennifer Johnston's jewellery rattled so much we had to take it from her.

Although it was a typically scorching Adelaide summer, the writers endured the heat of the lights for filming, and each spent half an hour patiently explaining the nature of their craft. The results reveal the authors as much as their work, from Nikki Gemmell's reaction to her first novel being accepted for publication – 'I just wanted to lie on the floor and wiggle deliriously' – to Thomas Keneally's 'Sometimes the novel dies beneath you like a horse, and when it begins to really smell, bury it. But not until it's really putrid do you bury it.'

Here are the distilled fruits of that process – twenty-four writers speaking about writing. We have transcribed their interviews, selected passages and edited lightly. There are also brief biographies of each writer and excerpts from their writing.

We hope readers find as much enjoyment and enlightenment in the reading as we did in the making of *Writers on Writing*.

James Roberts, Barry Mitchell, Roger Zubrinich
Adelaide, June 2001

fay weldon

Fay Weldon was born in Worcester, England in 1931, and lived in New Zealand for a time before returning to England. Her first novel, *The Fat Woman's Joke*, was published in 1967, and since then she has written numerous novels, collections of short stories, and drama for television. Her novels include *Down Among the Women, Female Friends, Puffball, The Life and Loves of a She-Devil, The Cloning of Joanna May, Life Force, Big Women* and *Rhode Island Blues*. She lives in London.

OK, it's 1983. Medusa is going great guns. Women have discovered, as they say, their voice, and their history, their literature. The concept of sexism has arrived in the land, as the concept of racism arrived a decade earlier. It doesn't necessarily mean people behave any better, but they have a vague idea of what the new parameters of good and bad behaviour are. The world is not yet female, the gender switch is not yet thrown, God is still the Patriarch, not yet shoved over on his throne by Nature the Matriarch, but we're on our way, for good or bad.

From *Big Women*

When I began writing I think the most important thing was to finish it – to get the thoughts out of my head onto the page in any coherent order. It's not an easy thing to do, and practice makes it easier. Then you begin to worry about content, about good or bad or what people will say, but firstly it is just that peculiar business of working out what's what.

What you need to succeed in writing, I suppose, is something to say that other people want to hear. Especially for a young writer, you have to have come to some formed view of the world. You can just recount your own life and it's going to be interesting to all kinds of people – indeed, the sexual behaviour of young men is always fascinating – and you don't really have to invent all that much. You just record an account and shape it a bit and you will have a book, and you may well get it published. That doesn't necessarily mean that you are a novelist. It means you can write this one good, popular, successful book, and good for you. But after that, you need to begin to shape your own knowledge of the world.

———

I never quite know what inspiration means. Some days you want to write, some days you don't. The days you don't you sometimes write better than on the days you do. I can't remember who said it, but what's the use of inspiration striking if you're not sitting at your desk when it does? Inspiration goes out of your head. It's a mixture of the impulse to write and just extraordinarily hard work, which at times is boring and sometimes isn't.

Readers would like us to be magic people. They always ask,

'Do you write regular hours or do you wait for inspiration to strike?' Partly they want you to have to be working really hard to get away with it, and partly they want inspiration because there's something magic about it, and that justifies them in spending good money reading a novel which is really nothing but invention and lies and exaggeration. People need all this sense of literature before they feel justified in reading. The whole vogue nowadays is for the writer to be connected to the book. People are interested in the personality almost more than they are in the book. You act being the writer. The writer is really some sort of boring, messy creature who just sits with a pen or in front of a computer and a pile of old rubbish drinking coffee.

———

If you have the idea and you're convinced of it, you should be able to make it marketable. You're part of a zeitgeist. If you're responsive to that, I think you'll probably end up writing what the market wants. Some writers sit down and write very good books because they know they can sell them. Other writers are obsessed by some idea which is completely unmarketable and will spend years of their life doing it.

I had no difficulty getting my first novel published. I just wrote it and they published it and that was that. Mind you, I had been writing television plays. Before that, I'd been working in an advertising agency, so I knew what was acceptable out there in the world. In a way you can make a novel about anything. It depends on how you can carry your reader along. The idea has legs if it goes on interesting you for 300 pages. If it doesn't, you don't write it.

Writing television drama had quite a lot of influence on my writing, and still does. I think I'm more conscious of a reader than many writers are. The way I develop a story or an idea is not exactly visual, but it moves in scenes. A wasted word is wasted value, if you like, on television. And you soon learn that and so you get quite a lean, economical style.

To listen to what you write is important. You have to do that terrible thing that you always hated doing at school, which is read it aloud. Write a paragraph and then read it aloud and make yourself listen to it, and don't believe that what you have written is sacrosanct, which many writers do at the beginning. They're so amazed that they've got it out of their head they can't bear to alter it. It's somehow not theirs any longer – it belongs to the page and they daren't alter it. But you have to get over that and go in there as an editor and shape and change and read aloud and take words out and alter, and in fact do this editing process. I tend to do a batch of about five pages and then edit, and then the next five and then edit, otherwise you get this feeling that behind you is this terrible mountain of error.

———

You need perseverance, courage, bloody-mindedness, a capacity for hard work, endurance; the kind of feeling that if they don't like it, fuck 'em, the feeling that you know better than they do. You know it's not quite true, but you have to have that particular feeling. Writers will write impossible things simply out of this feeling that what is forbidden must be all right. But you have to moderate that so that you have a degree of defiance – but not too much – and then you can push things just a bit.

I think you have to be born to it. Of course it's hard work. It's terrible, it's intolerable, it's awful. You can't wait to get it out of the house. It's crude to say it's like giving birth, but there is this sense – you want the midwife to wrap it up and take it away quickly, then come back and tell you how clever you are.

————

Style is really a matter of economy – the way in which you individually manage to contain the content in as few words and as gracefully as possible. That is style and that differs from writer to writer, and how you do that is a style which should be recognisable on a page. You can open a novel and say this is by somebody or other, if you're accustomed to reading. But as I say, I think it's a matter of economy; it's how you fit meaning into language, and it differs from person to person.

A: Well now, you ask, what is this thing called love? To give you a simple answer – love is enough to make you believe in God. It is the evidence you need which proves the benign nature of the universe. Love heightens your perceptions: it makes the air you breathe beautiful. It lets you know you are alive. It makes the news on the radio irrelevant; it turns the television into flickers. Love places you in the very centre of the universe; the knowledge that in your lover's eyes you replace God can only be gratifying. It makes you immortal: love, after all, being forever. It makes you vulnerable as a kitten in case you're wrong, in case love is not forever. One booted kick from the real world, you fear, and splat will go the kitten's head against the wall, and that's you finished. Yet fate weaves its heady patterns all around, good luck attends you, nobody boots you. That's what I mean by love.

In Darcy's Utopia all men will believe in God and all men will be capable of love.

From *Darcy's Utopia*

It's very hard to sustain interest in a novel, either writing it or reading it, in the first person. Of course it can be done. You the writer can never be cleverer than the 'I'. You can never know more, it constrains you quite a lot. Third person always needs more editing because it's not colloquial narrative, which first person normally is. Of course you don't have to write a whole book in the first person – you can write some of it in the first person, some of it in the third person. The whole meaning of the book can be what the author knows, and what the author doesn't can be what the other characters know. I think first person is easier. First person is rather slack and idle; there's too much of it, too much 'I', too much present tense, these days.

———

Where to begin? I don't know. You get better at it. You know there's a back story; you have somehow to start at a point where you can easily slide that in without it appearing too obvious. An awful lot of people start their novels with somebody sitting at a window and then crossing the room, and you feel that's just because they're working their way into it and they don't honestly know where to begin.

I like a good opening sentence. I like an opening paragraph that actually means you have to write another 300 pages before it's explained. So that within that first paragraph, within that first page, there is so much material, you have set so much up for yourself, that it takes you there. It's like the first sentence of Jane Austen's *Emma*, which I can't remember now, but it was about Emma who had everything that anybody could possibly want and yet . . . You know what's going to happen next, you want to know what happens to her, and then on you go. So you need to set up your proposition at the beginning.

That's what I mean when I say that you need to have a world view before you begin to write. The novel is really a formalising of your experiences and a fictionalising of them, and finding the sort of personification of it and then moving this into other people's heads so that they know more than they did before. You begin with what you think you know and what you believe other people don't know yet.

You know your initial proposition, if you're me. Sometimes you know more, it depends what you're writing. I wrote a detective story, a sort of thriller, once – you need to know more or less what's going to happen before you begin. Other novels are more organic and you don't know what's going to happen next, except you know what your proposition is. You have set your characters up somehow properly, you then put them together and you see what happens. With any luck those novels tend to be a bit shorter. I find at around 216 pages the knot ties and unravels again, or ties itself up in some different pattern and your novel is there. You do that by the grace of God and the skin of your teeth, but it's more fun writing like that.

———

I've been sued, and publishers always settle out of court. The difference between journalism and fiction – journalism you have to speak the truth or they sue you, and in fiction you have to not tell the truth or they get you for libel. The transition is often quite difficult for people. But if people don't invent themselves, they don't understand the capacity for invention and they assume that you're *describing*. But you are, if you're me, *inventing*. Occasionally you describe and hope to get away with it. Mostly you do – that's rather wicked.

———

I think you get to know your characters by being that character, by acting that character. Writing drama helps you do that – even writing television commercials. The early wisdom was that you should be able to tell from any dialogue exactly who's speaking, because it will be different from the way that everybody else speaks. You simply *are* that person, which means you have to be as bad as your bad people and as self-justifying as a particular character. Fictional characters aren't real people. Fictional characters you can recognise. Real people are not consistent, either in their appearance or their behaviour. Put them in a different setting and you've no idea who they are.

If you write radio, you reveal things about people as it occurs to you, as a need arises. If you try and work out rationally what the listener knows that you haven't told them, you can't do it, so you disclose information on a need-to-know basis, and I think in a way you do that when you write novels. Some people write descriptions of characters, or know what they're like before they begin. That's a sort of script-editor habit, and is based on the therapist view of what human beings are. Fictional characters don't seem to me to be like that. But all writers are different. They all write in a different way. I may not be very good – I mean my characters may be more schematic than they should be because I'm kind of using them rather a lot to make a point – but that's the way I write.

———

Publishers are always looking for new writers of whom they can be proud and who will make them money, so if you have any sense you'll give them a manuscript which is finished and for which you can argue for every single word. Publishers are the conduit which leads you to the reader, but they're quite powerful.

Your real relationship is with the reader. You are writing for a reader, not a publisher, and that you have to remember. But at the same time you have to realise the reality of the situation, which is that the publisher is a sort of intermediary point and you can't do anything that will offend or upset or annoy or suggest to them that nobody out there is going to read this – and they often know best, I'm afraid. So you produce the best, remembering that your relationship is with the reader, remembering that you ought to publish a book that doesn't need editing; that's your purpose. You give them the novel that you think doesn't need editing. They may have a different view of it, but this is what you do – you give them a perfect work.

I once had two editors and if they both said the same thing I believed them. But they didn't often. The editor is another person you really need to know. That said, I'm a rather idiosyncratic writer and do things in a particular way, and if you try to intervene it makes matters worse. So it varies from writer to writer. For some writers editors are terrifically important. You may well need a sounding board. I prefer not to have a sounding board, but then I've been doing it quite a long time. I say that and I'm sure my editors would throw up their hands in horror, saying, 'What ingratitude after all the work I've done.'

I don't think writing is a career. I don't think you can see it as a career. It's just something you do. It's something you want to do. You want to put the world in words, on the page, and hand it over to other people. If you don't want to do that, don't do it. Okay, so in the end it's how you earn your living, but there are, by God, easier ways of doing it.

vikram seth

Vikram Seth was born in Calcutta in 1952 and completed his education at Oxford and Stanford universities. He has published a number of compilations of poetry, including *The Humble Administrator's Garden, All You Who Sleep Tonight* and *Beastly Tales from Here and There*. He has published three novels, the first of which, *The Golden Gate*, is a novel in verse consisting of 690 sonnets. The second, *A Suitable Boy,* achieved notoriety as the longest English-language novel published since the seventeenth century. His most recent work is *An Equal Music.*

The branches are bare, the sky tonight a milky violet. It is not quiet here, but it is peaceful. The wind ruffles the black water towards me.

There is no one about. The birds are still. The traffic slashes through Hyde Park. It comes to my ears as white noise.

I test the bench but do not sit down. As yesterday, as the day before, I stand until I have lost my thoughts. I look at the water of the Serpentine.

From *An Equal Music*

I would feel I'd failed the character in the book if I didn't describe their world reasonably accurately. If, for instance, a reader in San Francisco reading *The Golden Gate* thought, Oh he's just glamorised it for an East Coast audience. Or if someone who lived in a small town in India in the fifties were reading *A Suitable Boy* and thought, This doesn't work for me. Then I would feel that no matter what praise you get from critics, or whatever your readership says about you, to some extent the book has artistically not succeeded – in fact failed. And that's because what I like to involve myself in is a fictive dream, and if you shred the dream, or pull out a thread or two of it, then the whole of it comes apart. But it's not a dissertation, it's a novel. The research has to be in the service of bringing some character to life, or bringing some aspect of the plot or the story to believability.

———

[On the four necessities] For a start, ignorance. If I'd known that *A Suitable Boy* was going to take me ten years, I don't think I would have begun it. I thought it would be a short novel, maybe 200 or 300 pages, mainly telling the story of a mother's search for a suitable boy for her daughter. But because it began with a wedding, her sister's wedding, and there were lots of wedding guests at that wedding, I became interested in their lives.

I suppose the second is curiosity, sustained curiosity. I allowed them into the novel and of course they partly dug their own channels through this rather broad bend.

The other thing, I suppose, is some sense of persistence.

I wanted to know how the novel was going to end and I knew that there was no way I could find out unless I actually wrote it. So as the goalpost retreated from 200 to 600 to 1000 pages and the end was not yet quite in sight, I just went on and did finally finish it.

And of course the fourth thing is a patron, if possible. I went deeper and deeper into debt, but I sponged off my parents, and if they hadn't allowed me to do that I just don't see how I could have put body and soul together. It would have been very difficult.

———

I'm not saying that writing is a question of being dragged along by a team of wild horses – clearly there is authorial control involved as well – but I don't feel that one can be entirely deterministic and impose one's foreseen structure upon a novel. It is an organic entity both as to its length and as to its complexity.

I think I had to allow that this particular novel was not going to be the sort of novel that I planned it to be. I certainly won't write something simply because people have asked me for a sequel or a prequel to one of my books. I feel that unless there's a compulsion to write, there's no point in writing. Readers can always tell when the writer's bored. So I'll wait. There are lots of false starts, sixty or seventy pages down the line you often find that this isn't working out, but I don't know how else one can write.

Each book, each novel even, seems to be inspired by a different germ. In the case of *The Golden Gate* it was through reading Pushkin – loving that verse form and the tone that

Bears out the usefulness of
listen/noting down overheard
conversations.

Pushkin used, sometimes light and sometimes so dark. So in a sense it was literary inspiration. But I knew that I wanted to write, not about St Petersburg 150 years ago, but California, because that's where I was studying at the time.

With *A Suitable Boy* I heard a little shard of conversation: 'You too will marry a boy I choose.' And that 'too' caused the novel to begin at a wedding, which of course meant all these guests, which meant that it was a different kind of novel. And with *An Equal Music*, it's looking at this man, this imaginary person staring at the water, so it's a very visual inspiration, for a very aural novel. In other words, there are no rules and I'm not sure in what form the muse will come, which shoulder he or she will tap.

> *'You too will marry a boy I choose,' said Mrs Rupa Mehra firmly to her younger daughter.*
>
> *Lata avoided the maternal imperative by looking around the great lamp-lit garden of Prem Nivas. The wedding-guests were gathered on the lawn. 'Hmm,' she said. This annoyed her mother further.*
>
> *'I know what your hmms mean, young lady, and I can tell you I will not stand for hmms in this matter. I do know what is best. I am doing it all for you. Do you think it is easy for me, trying to arrange things for all four of my children without His help?' Her nose began to redden at the thought of her husband, who would, she felt certain, be partaking of their present joy from somewhere benevolently above.*
>
> From *A Suitable Boy*

Even if *The Golden Gate* had just sold one copy, at least I would have finished it, and I would have been pleased to have done it. I thought it wouldn't sell, and if you look at it sensibly there's no way it should have sold. People don't like reading poetry and certainly they wouldn't like reading 300 pages of poetry. For me too, before I began reading *Eugene Onegin,* the idea of a novel in verse was a sort of odd and inedible hybrid.

With *A Suitable Boy* it was far too long to be a commercial success, and now I've just stopped double-guessing the market. I'm just content when the market buys me – market meaning readers, individual readers.

On the other hand, there are certain writers whom I love to read who obviously were very concerned about the market. Take someone like Dickens, for instance, or other writers who published serially. The thing is, that as long as you're not only concerned about the market, as long as your primary interest is your characters and your story, then I think it works. Many good writers write mysteries or books set at racecourses – for instance, Dick Francis – and I love reading his books. So there it is – no particular complaint about writers who write for the market. I am, after all, part of that market.

––––––

I've actually had both writer's cramp and writer's block. I keep in reasonably good health, so I was really quite indignant when I found that my hand had become like a claw when I was writing *A Suitable Boy.* As for writer's block, very often when I'm writing something that I began in great hope, suddenly, some pages down the line, I find that the idea, the impulse, has fled. And there's this wall and I can't dig under it and I can't go around it and I can't jump over it and I can't break it down, and after a month or two of trying I sometimes just put it aside – it's not working, that kind of writer's block. But then the other kind, which is not knowing what to write – that I take as a necessary part of the job of being a writer. There will be periods when you'll just lie low and not know what's going to happen, where your ideas will come from.

———

Mrs Rupa Mehra, the sort of matriarch in *A Suitable Boy*, was based very much on my grandmother. Her nose used to redden, she would try to manipulate her family; she used to say, 'Only when I'm on the funeral pyre will you think of what I was trying to do for you and the sacrifices I've made.' She unfortunately never saw me put pen to paper, let alone finish that novel, but I dedicated it to her memory and also to my parents, who are living.

Now, in the case of my parents, there're some aspects of Lata, the heroine, which resemble the early life of my mother, but not many. Whereas my father does resemble one of the suitors. So let's say there are different degrees of resemblance. One of the things that happens in a novel is that even when you base a character on a particular person, in the course of the novel they meet people they wouldn't have come into contact with in real life, and so they change, as do the people whom they've met. And of course there are other people who are just characters you've read about, or composites, or bits and pieces of yourself flung around here and there. I don't think you can light up a character from within unless you invest something of yourself in them, and you don't have to be an adulteress who's just had an abortion in order to write about them.

I don't think one should inquire too closely about one's own connection with those characters, otherwise you become very self-conscious. You can't *be* them. There are certain kinds of novelists that can get away with style and structure and all the other things that school teachers like to talk about, but character for me is at the heart of the novel. You've got to be involved with your characters. You can't find them boring. If you find them boring, forget it. If you're in love with them, fine, but if they are full of religious intolerance and prejudice and are willing to start riots with people of different denominations or different religions, you can't very well love those characters, but you have to try to understand them internally, and to some extent you have to try to be them. If you're writing a novel in the first person, you're stuck with the character, and that character's blindness and that character's percipience and that character's views about all sorts of things.

———

It's very nice to have direct contact with your readers sometimes. But if you find that you're answering stacks of letters, and that takes up your whole morning, then you have very little energy in the afternoon for writing or even thinking. If you find that you're spending a whole year of your time – having written a book which may have taken two years to write – promoting it, then that seems to me to be a disproportionate amount of time.

On the other hand, if your publishers are getting behind you and are willing to spend the money, and if you don't have a patron and you have to earn your bread from your last book, and you don't know when you're going to write your next one, then one has to take a commonsense view of things. You've got to balance the periods of inspiration against the periods when you're basically just being, you know, a smiler, a signer, a speaker, and travelling around the world.

———

I finished writing the first draft of *A Suitable Boy*. I hadn't shown it to anyone until that point, but I thought that a few people should now have it inflicted upon them, and one of them obviously was my agent. I sent it to him in the only receptacle that would actually hold 2800 pages of double-spaced type – a whisky carton. He got it and he wasn't very well at the time, luckily. I'm not sure this improved his spirits initially, but what it meant was that he was able, from his sick bed, to take out a page at a time and read it. I'm not sure he would have had the tolerance to read it if he'd been at his desk.

I told him that it was a rough draft and I wanted his advice. I wanted advice from family and quite a few general readers. At that stage I sent it out quite widely – you can imagine the photocopying costs – and I waited for their responses. I didn't read the book again for another six months. When I had all the responses I read them very carefully. There was a mixture of points of correction, which I almost always took cognisance of, and then masses which were more of taste, which I had to balance as I was going through my book again.

I revised it, cut out about a quarter of it, and stitched the other parts together. There were parts which I cut out which were perfectly good writing but didn't have any place in that particular book, in the curve of that book.

So I think revision is crucially important, but I think also that eventually one shouldn't take the advice of people in positions of publishing power other than for reasons of good sense – that is, if they make sensible suggestions. You're very lucky to have that sort of editor who might work well with you. I think with *An Equal Music,* for example, the best suggestor was in fact from an editor, an American editor.

———

I don't have any particularly useful advice for young writers starting out. After all, I spent fifteen years of my life studying economics. Now, if I had had any advice to give myself I think I would have maybe spent five years doing it instead of fifteen. I would say one has to follow one's own voice, finally. There's no point being in love with the idea of being a writer. What motivates you must be that which you are writing about. I didn't know I was a novelist until I wrote *The Golden Gate* and was really involved in writing about the lives of these people living in California in the eighties. So, I would think, try as far as you can to write the first draft on your own, so that the arc of the short story or the novel isn't distorted by other people's advice. But having written it, take advice as widely as you can and then just weigh it up yourself.

anson cameron

Anson Cameron was born in Shepparton, Victoria in 1961. He attended Monash University before working in an iron mine in the Pilbara. Anson's short-story collection *Nice Shootin', Cowboy* was shortlisted for the 1997 Commonwealth Writers Prize. His novel *Silences Long Gone* was shortlisted for the 1999 NSW Premier's Award for Fiction. His most recent novel is *Tin Toys*.

The thing that draws him away from the Outstation most often now is his occasional need to sit in company and not tell his story. There are days when he convinces himself his story is all the world will ever know, even if he doesn't know it. Days when the need not to tell it rises in him and he climbs into his Land Cruiser and drives out of the forest to riverfront pubs to drink quietly at a bar while the young men and women of the farms and towns drink around him and wonder at him and maybe, in their cups, venture to ask him about himself. Either he will go downriver to the Barmah pubs or upriver to the Tocumwal pubs. And he will sit in their chilled, fermenting air beneath giant Murray Cod with their mouths agape, caught a World War ago and hung high on the walls and now wizened and yellow inside their varnish. On the wall below which fish are the black-and-white photos of the now dead men who caught them, wearing felt hats and white cotton shirts with the sleeves rolled high up their thin biceps and baggy trousers held up by braces, swayed back and straining hugely with the effort of holding these leviathans victoriously aloft for the photograph. And grinning wildly about every fish held victoriously aloft. Until they held them all aloft. Victoriously.

From *Tin Toys*

I'm not sure you can be taught to write. I've never been to a writing course or engaged in any sort of reading about how to write. I think the way to learn to write is to read the great books. Read everything good so you know what's possible. Once you know what's possible, begin to write.

It's also the case that you don't know what you know until you begin to write about it. Writing is a great way of thinking about a subject, and when you focus in on it and begin to write about it, you find that you do know quite a lot about a lot of things that you hadn't suspected you had knowledge of.

The most important thing when I began writing was getting a quantity of work done every day. It's getting a page or two out of yourself that fills you with confidence and allows you to spread your wings. When I started off I was happy to get a number of words out each day. The quantity was as important as the quality – the quality feeds off the quantity in the beginning.

Apart from perseverance, and bloody-mindedness, I

think you need to find your own voice. You need to say the things you have to say the way you say them, not the way someone's just said them before you.

I can't just wait for inspiration – I'm too old. I have a full-time job and children and so I have to find a time and place to sit down and actually start writing. When inspiration does come to me it comes more or less in the negative. Most writing is a complaint about the way things are. It's the way the world is and the things that are wrong with it that usually inspire me.

———

I've had a lot of blue-collar jobs that take no thought or passion. When I'm doing them I think about writing. I'll rush off to a quiet room in the factory or the car yard I'm working in and I'll write a few pages on a bit of old hand-towel and take it home. Then when I sit at my desk and write on a laptop, I'm surrounded by little scraps of paper. My desk is world's-best-practice dishevelment.

I never think about the market. If I impress myself I just take it as read that it will impress the world, or I hope that it will impress the world. I don't try to second-guess the marketplace or I'd be writing blockbusters.

When I write I more or less have a shape, but I don't plot at all because you learn so much along the way. I sort of meander – it's a journey navigated by intuition. It's a hard way to write because I come to the computer screen most days not knowing where I'm going next, and that's rife with despair. The times when I know what's going to happen and where I'm going are the times when writing is easy and I'm banging out words fast. But not having plotted the book is not good for your psychological health. I'm not recommending it, but to let the characters and the situation and the ideas evolve seems like an honest way to write.

I become subsumed by characters. If I'm writing about Hunter Carlyon who is black, I try and immerse myself in the hostility and the racism that he's known and bear that in mind wherever he is and whatever he's doing. Writing has a lot in common with acting – you act out your character's role, you have to imagine yourself as someone else. Dialogue gets close to the bones of humanity. Oftentimes you can tell people things through characters and through their specific dialogues in a better fashion than you can just by observations. When I first began writing I found doing dialogue very confronting because dialogue is actually pretending to be someone else. I also found it very confronting because people who are somewhat similar to yourself are doing the talking when you first start writing.

———

A first sentence is one of the most enjoyable things you can do. Ending a novel is a lot more difficult. Readers usually want closure – they want a rounded circle and things to make sense and the journey to be complete, which is sometimes a dishonest way to represent life. You know life's not really like that, so I struggle with the endings of my books. I sometimes know where they're going to end and sometimes I don't. I have no advice to give on that subject apart from saying, Just sit down and think about it and come at it from a few different angles.

———

I redraft and rewrite in a totally haphazard fashion. If I'm at where the action is happening now and I need to change a fact back in the text somewhere, I do it. If I go back into the novel and I find something doesn't quite ring true, I'll begin work there and I'll traipse back and forth across it with no plan until I think I've got it right. Some parts might need practically no revision, and other parts I might revisit ten or fifteen times, and then the editor might revisit them a couple of times as well. I just bang away at it until there comes a point where I say, Yeah, that's right.

So the plump girl whose breasts hang astride the cue as she shoots her pool, and the tattooed boy with cutoff sleeves who is playing against her and always positions himself opposite her when she stoops to shoot, and the bikers loud out in the beer garden, and the local cricket team in its variegated creams, and the farmers with their wives and the truck drivers with their poker machines, they all wonder. They are all dying to know his story.

He drinks there believing he is the star in a sort of theatre of wonder. Sits there imagining people yearn to know about him. Sits there revelling in the perverse satisfaction of not telling his story. Letting them nudge each other and whisper behind their handbacks their speculations and their fanciful theories as to where this man's epic tale begins and ends. Sits there telling himself, That's right, stare and wonder. Because I have a story all right. The bloody story. I could tell you the whole dirty trick of life. But you just wouldn't get it. Yeah, look at me. I'm one of the world's great repositories of wisdom. And I'm old and bent and dying. I'm the Alexandrian Library in full conflagration. And the heat is just too intense for you to retrieve a single book.

From *Tin Toys*

I'm not conscious all the time of my style but I am conscious of a certain idiom and a certain resonance in the background that's got to be special to me and not to anyone else. But that doesn't affect any conscious act. I don't write a sentence and say, That's a good sentence but it sounds a little bit like someone else. The writing just comes out, but subconsciously I'm aware of the need to keep a clear voice and not be subsumed by some far-flung academy of writers.

There are poker machines and cheap Russian vodka and rodeos, and things that people could be doing other than reading my books, so I'm constantly aware of pace. I do go back and say, This is a good idea and there is a resonance; there might be a point but it's taking too long, so I have to compact it or add something new. The reader deserves entertainment, so I try to keep it moving.

———

When you lose confidence in your work, keep writing. The easiest option is to walk away and to get some space and time, but you should try and write through it. You'll get something good every day. It might only be a couple of sentences – it might only be a thought or a good comment from one of your characters, but you'll usually come up with something in the course of a day's writing. If you shied away from writing every time you worried about your abilities and where your work was going, you'd get half the work done you should be getting done. Writing's like anything else – there are good times and bad times and you've got to write your way through the bad times to enjoy the good times.

I think the hardest thing about writing is the thought in the back of your mind that you're expending all this emotional energy and intellect and that it might all be worthless. Sometimes I suspect that books don't change the world very much, and at other times I think they've got the power to change people. I think most of my moral and ethical makeup comes from books, but there are many hours when you're writing a book when you wonder, What's the point of it all?

It's a long road and you've just got to keep banging away at it and enjoy it. If you're not enjoying it, if you're looking at the prize and not the actual work at the end of it, then you're going about it the wrong way.

———

It wasn't hard to get my first book published. I had a collection of stories that had had some success with competitions and were published in small magazines. I sent them away to a woman I used to know socially, an agent at Curtis Brown. She loved the work, and within a couple of weeks she'd sold them to Pan Macmillan. She'd also sold a novel that I hadn't yet written.

Still, there was a lot of writing that went before I first got a book published and there's a bit of luck involved. My publisher has a stack of manuscripts in the corner of her office as high as a Great Dane and just as long. She can't read them all – she gets

so many sent to her – so that's an awfully hard way to get published. I think you've got to go through an agent. They act as a
filter for the publisher – they're not going to send anything to
the publisher that they don't think is publishable because
there's just no profit in it for them. Having said that, agents get
a lot of stuff sent to them as well, but I would start sending
things to agents rather than publishers. Publishers get hun-
dreds of manuscripts every year and they obviously can't read
them all.

―――

Writing, when you're doing it well, is a lot of fun. You hear
about what agonies it entails, but when you're writing well it's
a joyous act, and you rise from your desk after a couple of
hours' work on a real high. So I would say to young writers,
Take joy and take pleasure from the act of writing. Keep your
eyes off the horizon and the prize, and enjoy punching out
the words.

robert drewe

Robert Drewe was born in Melbourne in 1945 and grew up on the West Australian coast. He is the author of five novels and two volumes of short stories, *The Bodysurfers* and *The Bay of Contented Men*. His novels include *The Savage Crows*, *Our Sunshine* and *The Drowner*, which won seven national prizes including the Adelaide Festival Prize for Literature. His most recent book, *The Shark Net*, is a memoir of his early life in Perth and has also won multiple awards. Robert Drewe now lives in Sydney.

> *It's a different sunlight – harsher, dustier, more ancient-looking –*
> *that enters courtrooms. Streaked by this ominous light, guarded*
> *by two big uniformed cops and hunched in his old-fashioned blue*
> *pin-stripe suit with the curling lapels, the prisoner looked different*
> *too. He was uglier, smaller, and, with the eyes of the courtroom on*
> *him, even more self-conscious than usual. He looked like a crimi-*
> *nal in a B-movie or in* Dick Tracy. *He really was the stereotype*
> *of a crook. Even so, for my own reasons I was having trouble fit-*
> *ting the headline* Maniac Killer At Large *to him.*
>
> From *The Shark Net*

I'm basically a fiction writer of course, but memory comes into everything you write. When you're relying on memory entirely, as you obviously do with a memoir, it's easier in one sense because you can set things down faster as you recall them. But it's simultaneously more harrowing, or it was for me, when you're dealing with family material, or when you're dealing with dramatic events in your life and the lives of your friends, as in the case of *The Shark Net*. So I found it quite a speedy process, but outside of the time I was writing it, it was on my mind more and in a more worrying way. I was more anxious than I normally am while writing a novel.

When you are drawing family members, for the reasons that everyone in the world appreciates, you are treading on eggshells. I tried to be absolutely true when dealing with my own family and myself. Hence the anxiety. But if you're going to do this you have to be scrupulously fair. You can't whitewash events. So that was one set of worries. But I was also dealing with a real murder case, a real serial killer with family who were still alive. And the victims' families were still alive. So I did feel a responsibility to treat all those people with scrupulous care, including the murderer's family.

The real events that *The Shark Net* describes are the murders of eight people in the late fifties and early sixties in my childhood and adolescence by one man, Eric Cooke, who briefly worked for my father and whose court case, at a later stage, I covered as a young reporter. One of the victims was a friend of mine. Another friend of mine, a close friend, had his tomahawk stolen one night by a prowler – the murderer – who then used it to murder someone. And my friend's fingerprints were on the hatchet.

So all these interwoven events took place, and my own friendships and so forth were bound up in them, as were a lot of feelings of many Perth people at the time. This series of killings became instant local myth. Even today, thirty-five years or so later, Perth people still speak about them as if they happened a couple of months ago. It changed the way the people of Western Australia saw themselves. It made them more suspicious, less innocent, less trusting. And all this was fascinating material to me. But I felt so close to it that for years I neglected to write it. It was easier to be more detached, to make up a complete novel rather than draw on these intense, familiar events.

In the 1970s I'd decided I was going to be a novelist, and make things up, and not resort to nonfiction ever again. But then, having written eight or nine books of fiction, I thought, Well, this is a bit silly, I can write nonfiction too. Let's tell a true story. The story of Eric Cooke is almost too strong for fiction. There are, however, imaginative passages in it that I created. Imaginative by necessity. The killer is now dead – he was hanged. I tried to imagine his feelings while he was doing some of these crimes and two chapters became a sort of informed fiction. But of course I knew him, and knew the events and had covered them and still had the cuttings and records.

I knew a lot about Eric Cooke, the murderer, and I read everything that had ever been written about him. I interviewed his wife and son, researched a lot of material on him from the past, and I had had conversations with him myself, of course. I drew on all that and tried to imagine, as you do as a novelist, what it was like to live with his deformity.

He had a harelip and a cleft palate, which had adversely affected his view of the world, but he was very athletic and spritely. I can remember him running up and down the steps of our house delivering things, and he was very nimble. He was a good sportsman. He was a surf lifesaver, played top-grade hockey, and was obviously a very good cat thief and stealthy prowler, so I just put myself in that frame of mind, if you like. It wasn't particularly pleasant but it was artistically quite satisfying.

The sound of a man clearing his throat woke me one winter morning. I heard him spit, then the scrape of his boots and a hissing noise. A high, sweet smell came into the bedroom. I peered out and saw a man crouched in the yard below the window. He looked like a lurker to me. He had a tank strapped to his back and a woollen cap in East Perth football colours pulled down over his ears. He was spraying our back path and stairs with liquid. It was barely dawn and steam was rising from the cold cement when the liquid hit it, and the liquid was running down the stairs and fizzing into the lawn. A vapour mist clung around the man's legs and waist. He frowned up at me and turned back to his spraying.

It was six-thirty. My parents were still asleep. I went outside in my pyjamas and stood there in his vapour. I didn't ask what he was doing but by standing there I was obviously wondering.

After a while he looked up from the mist and said, 'Poisoning Argentine ants, aren't I?'

> *'Have we got Argentine ants?'*
>
> *He was spraying so vigorously the poison was splashing as it hit the cement. It was running down the path and pooling under the clothesline and trickling down the stairs into the Doghouse. It smelled like fly spray but sweeter, like DDT mixed with honey. 'Dunno,' he said. 'But I'm spraying for them anyway.'*
>
> From *The Shark Net*

In my mid-twenties, I was playing in the park one Saturday afternoon with my small sons, and I was working as a journalist, and I had a sudden urge that what I really wanted to do was write novels, and I would do so. I would stop what I was doing and begin writing immediately. So I did. And it was quite risky, financially. Fortunately I was able to give a couple of months' notice and get my affairs in order, and we just lived in a rented flat, so it wasn't as if we had a mortgage to pay off. I couldn't afford to have a mortgage to pay off.

So I wrote the first book, *The Savage Crows*, on the kitchen table at night, and after that Gough Whitlam became prime minister and the Australia Council was formed and the grant system started, so with the second book I was able to get an Australia Council grant, and like my whole generation of writers, that saved my life really. So that was how it all began, with an epiphany in the park on a Saturday afternoon – with a hangover probably.

The Savage Crows centres around a young man's obsession with the genocide of the Tasmanian Aborigines, which was an interest of mine at the time. The term 'postmodern' wasn't known to me then. Rather than write a simple historical novel,

I thought I'd take it a step further. I'd write about someone writing about writing an historical novel, but also using historical material that I'd researched and knew about. So that's how I handled it. I didn't really know what I was letting myself in for. I didn't know how much research I would still have to do or I probably wouldn't have begun it. I wouldn't write a book like that now, but I didn't know enough to know that it was hard to do. To read it now is reasonably embarrassing, but I can still see the earnestness and hard work and remember the high instincts which were probably more political than literary. The literary part came later.

———

Books take such a long time to write – well, they take *me* a long time to write, up to about three years, so the last thing you want to do is to turn around and do something exactly the same. Part of the ploy is to keep yourself entertained for as long as you possibly can. If you can't do that, then you don't have much hope of interesting anyone else. So I'm keen on doing new and different things.

I like the idea of doing a book of stories, say, between novels, or in this case a memoir, or nonfiction, and, if I am writing consecutive novels, for them not to be from the same time period or written in the same voice. That's just human nature, not to want to repeat yourself. It's like painting the walls of your house – after you've done three yellow walls, you can't wait to get onto the blue one.

———

Find an agent. The romantic days of throwing a manuscript over the transom really don't apply. Go to a good agent and convince her to read the book and then get her to make the submission. That's what I would do, because publishers will still look at a reputable agent's submissions. The usual things apply – type legibly, double space and all that sort of thing. You would think that's obvious but it isn't. Every second story I've judged in competitions is single-spaced, and it drives you crazy. Why start off at a disadvantage? What are you trying to do? Save money on paper?

And if you're writing on a computer, resist the urge to illustrate the manuscript with flowers and decorations and smiley faces, because that will annoy the publisher, unless you're a nine-year-old girl. So just write plainly and clearly and go to an agent. Don't submit it until you know it's really as good as you can make it. While spelling mistakes and things aren't vital if the book is fabulous, they're important if no-one's ever heard of you and you're trying to convince them that you're good. These days, with spellcheck and what have you, spelling mistakes shouldn't happen.

––––––

If you want to write novels, get another job, not necessarily anything to do with writing. There're probably as many novels to come out of waitressing as journalism. It doesn't matter what the job is, the important thing is to write all the time, at night or whenever you've got a free moment. In the morning before work. Regularly writing is what makes you better. And reading widely and well. Don't read only the people of your own generation and interests so you can write yet another urban, streetwise novel. They're fine, but there are a lot of them being written and already the vogue is on the wane.

Publishers are astonished when someone in their twenties doesn't want to write about sex, drugs and rock 'n' roll. It's worth bearing in mind that originality is the point. If you want to be a writer because it's fashionable, or you want to write fashionable things, then you're probably doomed.

Just keep doing it, writing daily, even if it's only jotting things down in a journal – jotting down what happened at the end of the day is the best way of doing it.

claire messud

Claire Messud was born in the United States in 1966. She was raised in Connecticut as well as Toronto and Sydney. She studied at Yale and Cambridge and now lives in Washington DC. Her first novel, *When the World was Steady*, was published by Granta Books in 1994 and was shortlisted for the Pen/Faulkner Award. Her latest novel is *The Last Life*.

> *The beginning, as I take it, was the summer night of my fifteenth year when my grandfather shot at me. In this way every story is made up, its shape imposed: the beginning was not really then, any more than was the day of my brother's birth, or, indeed, of mine. Nor is it strictly true that my grandfather shot at me: I was not, by chance, in the line of fire; he did not know that I was there. But it was an event, the first in my memory, after which nothing was the same again.*
>
> From *The Last Life*

I always wanted to be a writer. Telling stories was something I always loved to do and always wanted to do. In high school and university, when I was writing, it was alongside school, but I suddenly became aware that I would go out into the world and I would be writing alongside what? You know, how to make a living, how to make a life. It's a matter of how to cobble together a life that doesn't compromise the work you want to do.

I teach and that's great up to a point, except it uses many of the same energies that writing does, so it's important not to be teaching too much or not to take on too many students. I have done journalism – it's a different sort of writing but it can use up a similar sort of energy. I know people who write for television or film and that too is a viable option, except I think that the lure of money can become so great that it's difficult to get back to the work that doesn't pay. So I think it's a matter then of finding the way to fit writing into a money-earning life.

———

I don't think about the market, but I'm sure it's absolute folly not to. It's especially true in the United States where, increasingly, chain bookstores have a say in whether books actually even get published. For example, when they're doing the numbers at the publisher before they make an offer, they call up Barnes and Noble and they say, 'If we had this book, what sort of order would you put in?'

I think this market-driven notion of publishing has really changed a writer's sense of place in the culture. I know people who have written a couple of literary novels and then their publisher has said, 'Well, they're not selling very well, so now you have to write a thriller.' So they have. And then the thriller does wonderfully well and they become thriller writers. I don't want to be a thriller writer.

My editors, both in Britain and the United States, have been very supportive, so I haven't felt pressured to do something for market reasons. But I do think the influx of big money into publishing has changed people's sense of what's possible. I don't think anybody used to think of writing as a money-making proposition and now they do.

———

I'm somebody for whom character is very important, both as a reader and as a writer. Place is also important to me. Those are the things I focus on in the beginning of my writing. Who are these people? Where are they? Those two things are inextricable. How are these people going to react to the circumstances and the places in which they find themselves?

It's amazing how many students I have who, when writing stories, say, 'He was tall with brown hair,' and that's the only description they give of the character. You say, 'Well, that describes several hundred million people,' and then they say, 'He had a brown suit.' Well, that doesn't cut out very many of those millions.

I often give this example. In *War and Peace*, Andrei Bolkonsky's wife Lisa is a very minor character who actually dies early on. She's described by Tolstoy as having an upper lip that's too short – that's the only physical detail you have. Her mouth is never quite closed. From that I can see her. Every time she enters the room I have a very distinct picture that is partly created by me – I have the detail that I need in order to create this person for myself. The reader's imagination is very important in the creation of a character.

The key, when you envisage the character in your mind, is to see the things about them that are distinct and particular. If you're sitting on the subway looking at the person opposite, you notice the wart on their chin, or you notice that their hands are disproportionately large, or you notice that they're wearing very strange shoes. You don't notice the things that are ordinary about them – you notice the things that are particular.

––––––

It's amazing how many of my students want to be writers but actually don't read. You do have to ask why, if you don't read, would you want to be a writer? It seems that the only way we can learn as writers is by reading for the craft, to see what's working and why it's working, and what isn't working and why it isn't working.

I also mean to read just for the sheer joy of it – to discover how many voices there are and what extraordinary stories there are. People sometimes think, I don't have anything to say, my life is quite ordinary. But as Eudora Welty points out in an essay, it's not that anybody's life is actually extraordinary, it's that everybody's voice is different. Every story has already been told but nobody will tell it as *you* tell it – nobody will tell it seeing what *you* see and observing what *you* observe. It will be your story just because you're telling it. So I think it's important to have a sense of that variety through reading.

––––––

My second novel is the only sustained work that I've written in the first person. I didn't find it difficult to imagine what it was like to be the narrator, in part because I think much of what she's describing is being a teenager, and everybody's been a teenager. It's a sort of ventriloquism. I don't know if I would find it difficult to inhabit the voice of an 85-year-old man. I think that probably would be a bit more difficult.

At dinner parties I'm always looking around and imagining what the other people are thinking, so sometimes I tune out of the conversation and lose my way. Making up stories and projecting them into other people's heads is something that I practise a lot.

Nabokov said, very grumpily, that anybody who said their characters go away from them was just not keeping sufficient control of them. He said that your characters were your own creations and they should do exactly what you told them to and nothing else.

In my first book – it's a novel about two sisters – I had an outline in which the two sisters, who are in different places for most of the novel, would meet at the end. It was going to be a happy meeting and a reconciliation. They hadn't seen each other for a long time, but now they would and they'd have things to say to one another. But when they actually did meet, they didn't have anything to say, and it became clear that their estrangement was going to continue indefinitely.

When the book was published people said, 'The ending's kind of depressing, I don't know why you had that ending.' I really had no choice. I realised that because of their characters and the things that they'd been through, and the circumstances in which they found themselves, they were not going to make nice with each other. So I think when you do create people and they do become real, you have to be true to them – you have to follow what they would actually say and do.

> *Those summer evenings were all alike. As Marie-José used to say, we had to make the time pass. Of its own accord, it didn't, or wouldn't: the days lingered like overripe fruit, soft and heavily scented, melting into the glaucous dusk. We gathered by the hotel pool, on the clifftop, after supper, watching the sky falter into Prussian blue, to blue-black, and the moon rise over the Mediterranean, the sea spread out before us, whispering and wrinkled. Every night the white, illuminated bulk of the island ferry ploughed its furrow across the water and receded to the horizon, the only marker of another day's passage.*
>
> From *The Last Life*

I revise as I go along and then when I have a draft. I know some people get everything down first and then revise later, but I sort of go back and forth.

I write by hand. I don't write on a computer because I type fast and it's too easy for me to put things down. I actually write very small and the pages are completely full, and so when I go back there are all these crossings out and then there are some asterisks and stuff on the backs of the pages. Then I put it on the computer, revise again, print it out and go through it. That's when the whole thing of entire chapters going, or big structural changes and moving things around happens. I can't really do that at the stage when it's all handwritten because it's too hard to read. I can only read it straight through as it's written when it's at that stage.

When it's on the computer and I have the whole thing, then there are probably three drafts after that, with sometimes fairly dramatic shifts and cuts and changes. Sometimes whole new characters come in or are taken out, so it's a long haul.

————

Writer's block can be fairly constant. At the same time it's pretty easy to get past. There was a story about a day-long course that was being offered about how to get over writer's block. You paid something like a hundred dollars and this guy at the front handed out sheets of paper and a pen and he said, 'I'm now going to lock the door. You're not going to leave here until you've written twenty pages.' That was how to get over writer's block and I think it's true – you just have to write.

I do find that constraints help. There was a French writer who wrote a book with no letter *e* in it. It's a murder mystery, and any time somebody's about to say a word with the letter *e* in it, they die. It's very entertaining, and very difficult to write, I imagine. If I give my students this exercise saying, 'Write for twenty minutes without using the letter *e*,' they stop asking, 'What will my subject be?' and they worry about not using the letter *e* and the story forms itself. I think that in the beginning, if you're blocked, and you set up some arbitrary box you have to sit in, something will come out of it.

————

A writer needs obstinate perseverance to succeed. Writing is a fairly thankless undertaking. I think people get tired of it pretty quickly, so sticking with it is the greatest part of the battle. That said, perseverance and the ability not to get downcast by rejection, which is certain and ongoing, is just part of the game – even when you're published. Bad reviews are a public rejection one has to take with grace, and some people don't.

———

I can't remember who it was that said that if you waited until the muse spoke you'd write for about three days in your entire life. I certainly think that routine is the key to writing – to find a way to be writing daily, or as close to daily as possible.

I try to work my life around writing, but I think it's such a more difficult thing for women to do than men, because I believe women are brought up to be always accommodating and agreeable. I remember saying to a roommate in college, 'Mark, none of the lights work in the house, we have to go out and get lightbulbs.' And he said, 'Please, Claire, I'm in the middle of a thought, I have more important things to think about than lightbulbs.' And I thought, Well, Mark, I have more important things to think about than lightbulbs too, but somebody's got to think about them. So I do think that for women it's important that we learn to say, I have more important things to think about than lightbulbs.

nikki gemmell

Nikki Gemmell was born in Wollongong and was a news broadcaster on the ABC's Triple J radio station for a number of years. She travelled to Antarctica in 1995, which inspired the setting of her first novel, *Shiver*. The follow-up novel, *Cleave*, about a journey in the Australian outback, was published in 1998 and *Love Song*, set in England, in 2001. Her work has been internationally critically acclaimed and translated into many languages. She now lives in London.

> *I can catalogue Antarctica by touch.*
>
> *The touch of air sucked dry on my cheek, the fur of a day-old seal pup, the touch of an iceberg, a blizzard, a lover, the touch of sweat at minus twenty-three, of a camera stuck to the skin on my face, of cold like glass cutting into my skin, of a snowflake, of a dead man, of a doctor's fingers on my inner thigh, of a tongue on my eye.*
>
> From *Shiver*

I'm one of these readers who goes into a bookshop and flips open the book, and if I'm not grabbed by the first paragraph or the first page then I'll put the book down because I just don't have time. And for me as a writer, I need in a way to have a distinctive voice – a unique voice – to write in a way that no-one else does. I want that to shine through in the first paragraph. I want to hit people in the gut if I can with my very first line. So it drives me crazy. I slave over the first paragraph and over the first chapter, not only to grab the agent, the first person who's going to read it, but to grab the publishers and then ultimately to grab the readers.

———

I've wanted to be a writer since I was a kid. I started writing short stories in my late teens and getting them published in my early twenties. I go back to them now and I can hardly bear to read them because they are just so horrible. But the voice – I can see that voice that I'm constantly striving for was there in a much cruder way, in a much more obvious way, and in a way that makes me cringe now. But I can see that way back then, a decade ago, I was struggling to find that voice. I'm still struggling, you know. I feel as I'm becoming older the voice is becoming more distinct, but that said, it doesn't come any easier to me.

I've spent the last two years working on my third novel. I've just finished it and I actually changed the voice completely in the last month. I showed my agent in London a near-to-final draft, and he said the thing that he loved about my first two books was that he felt very close to the protagonist and he could empathise with them, and this one was not drawing him in. I thought, God, what does he want? He wanted me to change the narrative voice completely, change it from third person to first person, and I just thought, I can't do it. But I was legally bound by publishers in the States to get this manuscript to them and so I had to do it. I sat down and in this last month I just went hell for leather, changed it completely, changed it into first person. It was like, I've found the voice, and after two years of trying I had it. And so the final reworking, even though it almost killed me, actually came quite easily.

———

I got so many letters, saying, 'You've been through so much, it was so raw and so honest,' but I had to say to people, 'This is not me,' even to my mother. I sent her a proof copy of the manuscript and she didn't ring me for about a week, and I thought, Oh my God, what does she think? Then finally she rang me and she said, 'Darling, I didn't know you were an alcoholic.' I just said, 'Mum, this is fiction, you know. I had to spice things up a bit, to make her a little bit more interesting, so I turned her into a bit of an alcoholic nymphomaniac, which isn't me.' But I can say it's not me until I'm blue in the face and people aren't convinced.

———

Perhaps I think visually because of my background as a radio journalist. One of the first things I was taught in my cadet-ship days at the ABC was that you tell a story, you paint a picture for the audience. What I've done ever since is con-stantly rip out faces from magazines and newspapers and also landscapes and things like that, so I've always got a visual reference of what these people look like. In a way, that gives me the bones of the character and then I flesh them out with bits and pieces of people I know.

> *She slows. On the track ahead there's a gathering of wedge-tailed eagles. Twelve or thirteen or fourteen of them are gathered Hitchcock-Hollywood around some scattered red meat bits. Proud buggers, they're right in the middle of the road. There's the standoff as the car roars up on them and Snip's forced to slow to a crawl as the last one pushes itself reluctantly into the air, flap . . . flap . . . flap . . . its strong haunches dangling . . . flap . . . flap as it abandons its precious dead roo for a temporary post in a desert oak. She drives on swiftly past the smell, and the wedgies watch and wait for the flurry of dust to move on so they can flap back down to their meat.*
>
> From *Cleave*

I also keep journals. When I was fourteen my English teacher gave us an exercise in class to start a journal and we all sort of groaned and went, 'Oh my God, the teacher has to read this, this is terrible.' We handed it in every Friday. It got me into the habit of jotting things down, and ever since then I've been like a bowerbird. I might be on a bus, or even during a movie, if there's a great line or something, I'll just scribble it down in the dark. I always carry my journals with me – I'm up to about number fourteen now and they're fuel for my fiction too. I'm constantly taking things from them to flesh out characters.

———

I was an actress before I was a journalist and I find that helps me, because as an actress you're taught to get into the skin of another person and to empathise with that person. So I find myself doing almost acting exercises with my characters. But for me personally, I find dialogue the hardest aspect in terms of writing and I don't think I've cracked that nut yet. In fact with my third novel I tried to write a whole novel without dialogue just so that critics couldn't say, 'Oh, her dialogue isn't up to scratch,' but it didn't quite work and I've had to put dialogue in there, but I slave over it trying to make it real.

The thing that I worry about when I write, and I think it's one of the hardest things to do, is keeping people's attention. I'm paranoid that I'm going to be boring and that people are going to get to page 50 and just put it down. One of my favourite writers is Tim Winton – I just love his narrative drive. I can remember picking up *The Riders* and starting to read it at eight o'clock one night and at four the next morning I was still there – I just had to finish it. So I'm constantly trying to pare back my writing and to increase the narrative pull of it, so that people are just going through it like a steamroller.

———

So many novels have been about journeys. Mohammed said all journeys are a fragment of hell, and you know fragments of hell can make great narratives. I've seized on two of the biggest journeys I've had in my life, a journey to Antarctica and a journey to Central Australia, so I guess I have this relentless gypsy in me that constantly pushes me from place to place. I guess that's part of that whole process of always seeking new journeys, looking at places with fresh eyes as fuel for my fiction.

———

I sent *Shiver* to a very prominent Sydney agent. All my hopes rested on this book, and she rejected it quite brutally and said it was unpublishable. I thought, I can't do it, there goes the dream, I'm not good enough. I was so disappointed I literally put it in the bottom drawer and thought, Oh well, back to full-time journalism. Then a friend of mine said, 'Never take no for an answer, there will be someone out there who loves this book.' So after several months I picked myself up and tidied the manuscript up a bit and sent it off to Jane Palfreyman at Random House. She took it in twenty-four hours. I'll never forget, I was working at Triple J and she rang me that morning and said, 'We want to publish it.' I felt like a little cockroach on its back on the kitchen floor. I just wanted to lie on the floor and just wiggle deliriously! The sweetness of that after the initial rejection – I'll never forget that. You know, nothing has ever topped that moment when she said, 'We want to publish it.'

———

You've got to have discipline and that drive and that hunger. It's a hellish job, the hardest thing I have ever done. You've just got to stick to it, and it's so easy to fall by the wayside. Write as if you are dying. It works. Imagine if you've only got a year to live or something. I think that's the best motivator to get you to do it.

With *Shiver* I was working full-time and supporting myself. I was single and I just didn't have time to take six months or a year off or anything like that, so I thought, How do I do this? How do I write my novel around full-time work? In the end I just had to turn myself into a hermit. I would write before work, before Triple J in the morning. In my lunch hours I'd go into a spare studio at work and scribble. I'd come home at night and work until about ten o'clock, and then on the weekend I just wouldn't go out, I'd write the whole time.

I'm married now and it's enormously difficult to make writing fit, because it's an incredibly selfish job – it demands solitude. All the time I take for writing I feel like I'm taking away from other people. Maybe that's a particularly female thing. Maybe male writers find it easier to demand that selfishness. I have a terrible guilt about it, but I still do it. In London, every couple of months or so, I hire a little cottage in Cornwall and I go down there for a week and solidly write for about sixteen hours a day – almost sleep the book. It's always a big thing with my husband because he says, 'You're leaving me for a novel.' I have to do it and he understands that too, but he grumbles. It's the only way that I will be able to write.

tom petsinis

Tom Petsinis was born in Greece in 1953 and immigrated to Australia in 1959. He is a novelist, poet and playwright. His most recent book is *The Death of Pan*, a collection of short stories, and his novels are the acclaimed *The French Mathematician*, *The Twelfth Dialogue* and *Raising the Shadow*. His play *The Drought* was shortlisted for the Victorian Premier's Literary Award. He lives in Melbourne with his wife and two daughters and lectures in mathematics at the Victoria University of Technology.

Again the cold stethoscope. The bearded doctor's warm breath is scented with chamomile. Holding my wrist, he concentrates on my fading pulse. But my heart is already given up its lifelong count, its collaboration with natural numbers. The only numbers it is now susceptible to are the imaginaries: it can grasp the meaning of the square root of negative one, feel the presence of the elusive i. *By tonight, it will renounce these for the transcendental, the mystical,* π. *And by tomorrow it will renounce even these for the holy zero. Black footsteps on the marble tiles. A priest leans*

*over me and places his bag on the sunlit bed. A pin of light darts
from the silver cross swaying from his neck. His fingers are crossed
in a tight knot. The golden hairs on the back of his hands disturb
me. Perspiration glistens on his lined brow. Flicking the bag open,
he asks if I am ready to receive absolution. Summoning what
little strength I possess, I refuse with a harsh no. This is the last
word I breathe.*

From *The French Mathematician*

Mathematics has always been an area of interest to me
because first and foremost I'm a lover of mathematics and a
teacher of mathematics. I'm also a great lover of literature
and the written word. And the two had been running in parallel for a number of years. I'd lecture my mathematics and
then go home and concentrate on my literature.

About five years ago I thought, These two great loves in my
life shouldn't be running parallel; it's about time they con-
verged. So I approached some people at Victoria University
where I lecture and I said, 'Look, I've got this idea of proposing
a Master's thesis based on an obscure French mathematician
by the name of Galois, but I want to do this as a novel rather
than as a conventional thesis.' Professor John McLaren, a great
supporter of Australian literature, said, 'Tom that's a com-
mendable project, I'll give you some assistance.' We were able to
push it through the research committee and the result was the
germ of the present novel.

The original structure of that thesis was very fragmented,
very disjointed. I tried to mirror the chaotic nature of the
young man's life by deliberately choosing such a narrative

structure. When I took this one step further and submitted it to publishers, they felt that perhaps something a bit more conventional was necessary – at least something a bit more linear to allow the reader into the life of the young man without too many assumptions about his life. So the final work was an extensive reworking of that original thesis.

I wanted to get away from traditional biography. I think in a traditional biography a lot of detail is important to set the times and set the character. Being a poet as well as a novelist, I'm very conscious of using language in a very precise and compressed form. For me the image and metaphors are very important in that I'm able to make resonances whereby a lot can be said or a lot can be evoked, rather than deliberately conveyed through a lot of detail. I wanted to get away from a traditional biography and have more of a poetical type of lyrical novel, which I think the finished product is.

I must say as a novelist I found the research somewhat irksome. The sheer slog of having to go through the material, not only the material about Galois, the young man in question, about whom not much was known because he died young, but the surrounding material – the political currents of the days, the social milieu, the prevailing cultural trends in Paris of the 1820s and the 1830s. I find all this somewhat compressing and somewhat burdensome from the creative novelist's point of view. But I persevered through that and picked out what I thought would be the encapsulating images of the time, whether political or cultural or social, and then constructed the mosaic around those images.

And now mathematics appears through the human condition, transforming everything, perhaps as poetry and painting elevate suffering to art.

A deranged man howls at me from a dark doorway – Pythagoras's clear voice teaches that all is number. A beggar accosts me, his arms amputated and a placard around his neck blaming Napoleon. There is an equation of a parabola in the pink scar stitching each stump. I hold my breath against the sulphurous stench rising from an open sewer circled by children – Euclid's pristine postulates exist only in a vacuum. Gradually, as mathematics imposes itself on the surrounding squalor and chaos, it restores my buoyancy, hope and sense of meaning in an otherwise meaningless world. And as I leave the suburb, my vision of the Polytechnic is brighter than ever, my faith in mathematics restored.

From *The French Mathematician*

The voice posed a problem for me. I tried third person and I found the third person gave it too much of a biographical feel. In recasting some of the earlier chapters into the first-person narrative I felt that the voice came out far more urgently because I am dealing with a very young, conceited, arrogant adolescent – an adolescent for whom the world revolves around his ego. When I experimented with the first person, this urgency and this rebelliousness of youth came through far more convincingly, and I felt that the chord was struck correctly in the first person. From there on I followed it through.

You can't rely on the muse, it's very fickle. For me, ideas that I might have interact with ideas that I might read about, something stirs me and then it's just a matter of being disciplined to sit down and give some sort of shape and form to these inner stirrings. I think the craft of writing is very much that. It is a craft and it does require discipline. As athletes train in order to perform well in the Olympic Games, likewise writers have to have that training to be able to sit down and have their quota of words at the end of the day.

———

Be passionate about the subject, first and foremost, because it is a grind, it's demanding, it's taxing. Be familiar with the subject and the times, either through research or else the immediate environment – the sights, the smells that convey powerful and concrete images and stirring writing. And be truthful and honest in relation to the material you are using, and have this sense of respect for the material.

One of my earlier collections, a long narrative poem, is based on my grandmother, who passed away some years ago. She was illiterate and yet she was able to tell me so many stories about her past, her background, and her time in northern Greece as a girl. I always respected and treasured her stories, and there was always a sense that these are precious things and they should be used when the time is right, and when they are used they should be used with that sense of respect. I think that's important in using material.

———

Not long ago there was a bricklayer working across the road. He started in the morning at seven o'clock and finished at five o'clock, and by the end of the day he had the front wall up. I was working on a poem that day and by the end of the day I was exactly where I'd begun. Draft after draft and I was facing a blank sheet. I said, 'Look at that, wouldn't it be fantastic to be a bricklayer – at least there's something concrete at the end of the day.'

It is frustrating trying to give shape and form to intangibles. The process has its frustrations, but there are the rewards when you're able to say what you want to say. Then there is a sense of liberation – that you've excised this demon that's possessed you for the day. I find that for me, once this liberation comes, I like to leave the word processor and go out for a ten-kilometre jog.

―――――

In working with the editors at Penguin I took their suggestions and criticisms on board, and the finished product, I felt, had a certain wholeness that was more consistent with the prevailing trends of the novel. As writers we become quite immersed in our material, and sometimes we're too close to it to see we've said a similar thing 200 pages further on. The editor is one step removed from the novel and they can often see things that are beneficial to the finished product.

―――――

I think any writer who is worth their salt was first and foremost a reader. I think we need to have this passion for the written word first and foremost, and if a writer is then to emerge, it will be a natural process out of the process of reading. I think writing and reading are so inextricably bound that you can't have one without the other.

hilary mantel

Hilary Mantel was born in Derbyshire in 1952. In 1987 she was awarded the Shiva Naipaul Memorial Prize for travel writing. She is also the winner of the Hawthornden Prize for Literature and is one of England's most acclaimed novelists. Her titles include *Every Day is Mother's Day*, *Vacant Possession*, *A Place of Greater Safety* and *An Experiment in Love*. Her most recent novel is *The Giant, O'Brien*. Mantel currently reviews for the *New York Times* and the *New York Review of Books*.

The architect who had designed the Ministry's new building had been given a commission to excel all the other strange and wonderful buildings of modern Jeddah. The building was to defy, for scale and cunning, the green giant of the Petroline building, and the Ministry of Labour's silver and chrome fantasy on Al Hamra Street. It was to exceed in strangeness, in denial of gravity, the flying tented roofs of the airport's Haj Terminal; it was to induce wonder and reverence, even greater awe than the pure white 3D triangle of the National Commercial Bank, which floats above Bagdadia lagoon.

From *Eight Months on Ghazzah Street*

I'm not one of those people who sits down at nine o'clock in the morning and writes chapter one and then smoothly continues. A book takes me years and years from the first idea to the execution of it, so it has to be put together out of scraps I've gathered over the years.

I know a lot about the book before I start writing, but I start with a little idea and then let it germinate. My last book took me eight years, really, from the idea to finishing it, but during that time I was making myself available for it. If something came along that resonated with that book, I'd make a little note. There's a process by which you almost become sensitised to your material – it almost seems mysterious the way you're led towards the things that you ought to be reading or conversations that you might strike up.

What I do is collect up my little notes over the years and wait until I think the book's ready to be written, and I'm ready to write it. Finding that moment is quite crucial, because at the time the idea comes to you, you're not always ready to write that book. You may have to change a bit, you may have to live a bit, and the idea of the book as well might have to go through various transmutations. Then the time comes when you think, Right, now's the time to do it. Then for me the writing process goes very fast, because I've been thinking about it, or it's been at the back of my mind. In my experience you can't push a book through before it's ready to go. That all sounds highly mystical and impractical, but then I have a method which has always worked for me, by which I actually go about writing.

The scraps of papers I've collected over the years may contain as little as a word, a phrase, a scrap of dialogue, a description, or just a few phrases that evoke a place that I think might relate to the book, but I don't yet know how. I don't ask myself questions about these notes because that comes later.

When I'm ready to write, I pin the notes up on notice-boards around my room and I leave them there. Every time I come into my workroom I see them. I may not consciously be thinking about them but they're there. And over a few weeks, more and more begins to build up around those key words. A couple of lines of dialogue might become a whole page, a description which is a few phrases might flesh itself out, and I might introduce the human beings into it and begin to see where it fits in the book.

Gradually I begin to shuffle the order around, and then I can see that the structure of the book is forming without my really having to think about it consciously. When that phase is through, I put everything into a loose-leaf folder. It's very important to me not to set the order early on, so I never write in a hard-spine notebook. All my pieces of paper, fluttering like leaves in the breeze, go into this folder.

I work straight from that onto the screen. I then write very fast. It's usually 80 per cent there, but of course what really matters is the other 20 per cent, which is the refining process – making sure that every word works hard, that every-thing extraneous is stripped out, and that I'm attentive to the inner rhythm of what I'm writing.

I think it's good practice to read out loud. If you can't say it, you shouldn't be writing it. I aim to build up a rhythm within a book. I get a rhythm going within a paragraph that then builds up into a larger unit. The reader is maybe never going to be conscious of that, but you hope that for them it's making the book sing – that this rhythm is making the book have a spring and a forward movement, rather than being static.

———

I've moved around quite a lot. I grew up in the north of England, went to university in London, moved back to the north, went to live in Botswana for five years, and moved on to Saudi Arabia and back to the United Kingdom.

The book you're writing may not relate to the place you're living in at all, and in fact usually doesn't. So you're making a complete world inside your head, which is in a way a sealed world, independent of what's going on day by day, and that's the place you have to go to when you sit down to write.

———

The first book I wrote, although it wasn't the first published, was a mammoth novel about the French Revolution. I expressed the hope that it would be a complete world for the reader. I hoped the reader could live inside it, like a big house, and walk around from room to room and introduce their own furnishings. I wanted to give the book scope for them to change opinions within it – to think on page 100, Well, that character really revolts me. But by page 600 to be saying, Yeah, I think I get it now, I think I understand why he is like he is, and by page 800 to think, Well, maybe I'm a bit like that too.

So the reading of the book is a two-way process. The writer brings to the book her own preconceptions, prejudices, all the baggage of her personality, and the reader brings to it the same baggage. It's a kind of constant negotiation between the two of you.

I try to infuse all through my books that sense of being in an interaction, so that there is a kind of equality between writer and reader. I give my readers quite a lot to do. Sometimes I suspect people have the complaint they don't know what's going on, but there's nothing worse than spoon-feeding a reader. That's condescending, and nothing makes people lose interest faster than thinking they've worked a book out. I want my readers to be involved with me, and to be working away too.

When I started writing, as I've explained, I started writing an historical novel. The historical novel is usually very conservative in form. No matter what its subject matter, it has tended to produce a very orthodox and very old-fashioned kind of narrative line.

When I began writing I was quite young – twenty-two. I'd read enormously but I hadn't met any writers. I didn't have theories about writing but I knew that this kind of very conventional, almost Victorian-style narration would not suit the story I had to tell. The story was about revolution, it was about reworking and reconstituting, and my chosen form had to suit that. My narrative was fractured. It was not an overview – it was not an omniscient third-person narrator all the time. I was splitting up the text between various narrators and at one point my characters seemed to say, 'Well, enough of this "he said" and "she said",' and they just dived into script form. So suddenly I was embedding a play in the novel.

And of course, the question in my head was, Can I do this? Will readers wear it? Is it acceptable?

I remember picking up a novel by Thomas Keneally – I think it came out in 1975. It's called *Blood Red, Sister Rose* and it's about Joan of Arc. For me, this was an absolute inspiration. He had an off-centre narrative, he had script form – he had a sort of underground take on events and a highly imaginative one. He was touching the mythic level of history, not just the top-surface events. Although my novel was very different in setting and in time and in scale, I really took heart from that. It's incredibly important at the beginning of your career to find someone who is a beacon and who says to you, 'Yeah, you know you can try that, that's okay.'

———

In *The Giant, O'Brien* there are two main characters, both of them real. One is the giant himself, a man called Charlie O'Brien who was eight foot tall. He was born in Ireland at the end of the eighteenth century, and in 1782 he went to London to exhibit himself as a freak of nature. He was the sensation of the season, but a year later he began to fall ill, and the famous anatomist and surgeon John Hunter decided that the giant would be a fine addition to his museum of specimens. After the giant's death his body was delivered to John Hunter. He was skeletonised and John Hunter hung him up in his private cabinet. A few years after Hunter's death the bones made their way into the public realm, and today you can still see the giant hanging up in the museum at the Royal College of Surgeons in London.

What I had was a macabre real-life story, but when I began to research into it, I realised that John Hunter was very well documented. The giant's a different story. What's known about the giant you could probably write on the back of your hand. For the writer of fiction it's an opportunity, because you have the licence to invent. And a giant is of course a creature with one foot in myth anyway. A giant emerges straight from fairytales.

In real life Charlie O'Brien was only twenty-one when he died. He probably had a pituitary tumour, which may have meant he was mentally backward and a heavy drinker. His bones apparently show the evidence of tuberculosis. So it was a very young wreck of a giant who was actually imported to London.

I've gone back beyond that to ask myself, What might an Irish giant mean? I constructed a kind of fairytale giant who carries with him the symbolic status of the body of Ireland and the body of Ireland going among strangers. He's a kind of hero and he's a bard. He describes himself as an aristocrat of height – he's a great storyteller, he's a phrase-maker, he's a sophisticated mind, he's the man of the Enlightenment with a foot in the realms of romance as well. He's also a good man. He's one of the few good characters I've ever created.

So I had a book of two halves really – one research-based, one imagination-based. But then the giant came along and hijacked the story. Hunter became a character in one of the giant's stories. Hunter, for him, is a kind of predatory figure, released from a fairy story so that he also has a kind of mythic life. So running side by side are the real events as we know them and what I take to be the mythic layer of those events.

———

I've written a novel set in southern Africa in the late fifties and early sixties. It was as much a research project as writing about the eighteenth century, and perhaps even more formidable, because if I got it wrong there were people who lived in those places at that time who would tell me I was wrong. You have to be aware that it isn't just the dim and distant past that requires research.

I approach research with a great rigour, and in fact I may be too bound by it. I've had to learn from book to book to let my imagination go. That was the hardest task for me. My advice to people who want to write my kind of book is to give yourself the time and really never give up on your source material. But when you've got your source material, be aware that only the tip of the iceberg must show on the page. Seven-eighths of your research is going to support your narrative. I hate those books where the bones are always showing through and the characters take two pages to get dressed in the morning because the writer's done her research on costume. She's done it, so she's damn well going to show you she's done it.

You have to be aware that your characters, in their world, take the exterior world for granted. They're not seeing it every morning. They're not going out thinking, Oh, the streets of Paris are filthy today. Because they're filthy every day. Your characters notice things when things change. At that point it's legitimate for you to describe and bring your research in – always supporting your narrative but never dominating it.

> *The Ministerial HQ was to suggest to the beholder a miracle compound of all the elements, of earth, air, water and fire; as if to convey the mysterious grandeur of the Ministry's activities, the transcendent quality of its paper shuffling. It must be better than anything the West could do; but it must also be Islamic. Glorifying God was part of the brief.*
>
> From *Eight Months on Ghazzah Street*

Writers need a huge measure of arrogance. Nobody else believes in you, so you've got to believe in yourself. You also have to work at some kind of self-containment. Don't go around pathetically showing your work to everyone who comes along, soliciting approval for it – especially not from your family and friends, because what you'll get is not their opinion of your work, but their opinion of you, phrased in a covert form. So I would say be prepared to serve an apprenticeship to yourself – work away in patience until you think your work is ready to show.

———

You have to be very clear, if you want to write, what place it occupies in your life. I'm afraid that if you're ambitious, it often has to have first place – it sometimes has to take precedence over human relationships and anything else. If you've got a book you really want to write, it comes first. Sometimes people say things like, 'I've always thought I'd write a novel if

I had the time.' But we all have twenty-four hours in the day, and it's just a question of how you structure your priorities. It's not easy.

The main thing is that you have to have faith in yourself and then try to manoeuvre yourself into the right place at the right time. Never talk yourself down – other people will be only too ready to do that for you. When you get the breakthrough, don't expect people to be glad. It's often said you find out who your friends are when you're unfortunate, but you find out who they really are when you have a piece of luck, like publishing for the first time. There is a lot of luck involved but you've got to put the effort in to back it up.

———

Don't let people tell you to write to a market. You write what you want to write, because by the time you've prepared your book the market will have changed. You have to have the courage of your convictions. Write the book you want to write, and, above all, never write down to a perceived readership – that's one of the first things my agent told me. I said, 'I have a book in mind and I don't know whether to write it the way I really want, or write it in the way I think will be more accessible and acceptable.' He said, 'My advice is always write the very best you can.'

christopher koch

Christopher Koch was born in Tasmania. Among his forebears are a Prussian architect, an English sea captain and an Irish convict. He has worked as a producer for the Australian Broadcasting Corporation in Sydney, and has been a full-time writer since 1972, winning a number of awards, including the Miles Franklin Award twice. His novels include *The Boys in the Island*, *Across the Sea Wall*, *The Year of Living Dangerously*, *The Doubleman* and *Highways to a War*. His most recent novel is *Out of Ireland*. In 1995 Koch was made an Officer of the Order of Australia for his contribution to Australian literature.

A line of gum trees rose at a distance, in the direction of the lake: tall, bare, wraith-like forms, with black, swaying foliage at their tops. Level emptiness here. Lichen-covered rocks and prickly green bushes. Fathomless dark beyond them, with a half moon above. I came to a halt by some banksias: crooked black spirits.

The air was thrillingly cold: the sky clear, a breeze rushing steadily from the west, its breath filling the land. One of the bushes was tossed about suddenly, so that I swung to look with my heart in my throat. I had a sense of some presence behind me – but there was nothing. Occasional noises: the croak of a water bird by the lake, and the stamping of our horses in the enclosure. One of Carter's dogs barked twice; I heard the sound snatched up the wind, and flung away for miles.

My head swimming with brandy, I passed water in the grass. Then I looked up.

The sky was so near, I grew giddy. The stars! Buttoning up my trousers, I reeled, and almost fell over. The Milky Way's white river arched so close above me that I exclaimed: its source might have been just behind the eucalypts. Vast, this blue-black sky, vast but not distant. No sky in Europe came so low.

From *Out of Ireland*

I published verse before I published a novel, and poetry remains my main interest, but I decided as early as the age of twenty that the novel was the chief form in this century and that I wanted to tell stories as well as write poetry. I think that the novel has replaced the epic poem or the narrative poem. I know there are people now writing novels in verse form. I don't think it works. I think it's very artificial to create long narrative poems. The novel can do everything that poetry can do, except the lyric poem. It can never replace the lyric, which is almost one heightened moment, but I want to do most of the things poetry does. I want to use metaphor and I also write prose for sound, which is probably a bit silly in this century since people are not reading aloud to each other any more, but if you read Dickens and quite a lot of the nineteenth-century writers, you'll find that their work is geared to cadence. That's what I enjoy, but it means that you take a long time over your work, I'm afraid, and publishers get very sick of waiting for the novel to be finished.

I began writing poetry and I used to paint watercolour landscapes. I actually earned my living for a while as a black-and-white artist on the local newspaper, but I had no real talent for painting. They say in art what matters is not what you put in, but what you leave out. I was out painting landscapes in Tasmania with a friend of mine, George Davis, who really was a professional painter and became a very good painter. I realised that when George did a landscape it all worked well and had a great deal of lyrical feeling. I was trying to find out what I was doing wrong and George said, 'You're trying to put everything in, and you can't do that in painting.' One day, when I was working on a painting out in the hills and trying to capture this scene, I just got sick of it, threw it down and wrote a poem instead. From that moment I was hooked; I'd found my form. So my main interest when I began writing was landscape and the feeling behind the landscape in Tasmania.

———

If what I'm reading in my own work bores me then it will bore the reader, and I don't allow it to bore me. A lot of the craft in writing is a matter of what you eliminate. As a painter you feel, for example, that the colours are getting muddy here, it's not clear. The writer should feel that. If something blocks up the works, if something is there that shouldn't be there, then you get rid of it. It's got to work within the context of what you are doing and not be foisted on the reader for no reason.

———

Usually I make a character from about three people. If you put about three people into the pot and add your own imaginary purposes, you may get a reasonable character. It doesn't work if you just base a character directly on one person, but if you can manage to mix elements from a number of people in the right way then you get a character.

———

I never consider the market. I'm afraid I'm very self-indulgent. I write what I want to write. What I do consider is the imaginary reader, who you hope is an intelligent reader. If you consider that reader, then probably there'll be a reasonable market for your work.

I'm not sure that a lot of novelists now are considerate enough of the reader. It's a matter of the attitude that's behind the writing. I remember liking writers – even writers like Dostoevsky or Balzac – who I felt were addressing me, and essentially, underneath everything, saying, 'This is going to be interesting for you.' I don't feel that with a lot of contemporary writers. It's as if they're saying, 'I don't care whether you're interested or not but this is pretty smart stuff that I'm doing here.' The reader won't like that. What I want to do is make the reader feel it's worth going through the door. That's not exactly the market, but it's the person you're addressing. The market will take care of itself then, one hopes.

———

The beginning is the only thing that is pure inspiration. *Highways to a War,* for instance, began from a very small image, rather like a poem. There was a cigarette in an ashtray that somebody had left on a table and they'd gone out of the room. The person who'd gone was never going to come back. I didn't know who the person was, whose cigarette it was, what it was about, but that was where it began. Beginnings are very enjoyable; the middle and the end are a lot harder.

———

I was a boy of eighteen and this man was one of Australia's greatest poets, dead now, called Roland Robinson. I brought Roland a poem to show him and he said, 'Don't talk about it, make me see it.' That's what I think you've got to do; you've got to make the reader see it. But I'm not just talking about visuals – I'm talking about putting them through the experience. If you're going to take somebody into a room where something is happening, I want them to see the room, to smell it. Not everyone writes that way. Some writers are dominated entirely by psychological relationships – Dostoevsky, for instance. And that's fine. That just happens not to be the way it is for me.

> *And I suddenly understood that terror of infinite space which had gripped Pascal. This made my brain swim as much as the brandy was doing; I took hold of the rough, corky limb of a banksia to steady myself, and began to converse in whispers with my double-goer – as I often do, in times of turmoil and dilemma.*
>
> Self: – *What is the true nature of this wilderness? Are Plato's*

immortal Forms behind its mask? To put it another way: does this southern emptiness contain those ideal presences which give meaning and solace to the North? Are they universal truths after all? *Is Beauty really* here? *Truth? Goodness? Justice? Here, where no human minds have ever conjured up such things?*

Doppelgänger: – *Perhaps not. Perhaps Chaos alone is sitting behind the mask: mother of Erebus and Night.*

This proposition created a sort of vertigo, and I began to lose my hold on existence. I wished to reject such a notion out of hand – and yet it was wickedly convincing, here among the rocks and banksia trees.

From *Out of Ireland*

I don't think a young writer can write about things that he doesn't know. The one thing a young writer has to offer is his own experience, but he's got to transform it. It's not enough to write the usual autobiographical novel, you've got to have something more to say and you've got to be interested in people. The mistake with a young novel is to write about oneself and one's own preoccupations, which seem enormously important then. But if you're interested in the world outside yourself and the people you've experienced in your short life, you might do something worth reading.

———

The hardest thing about writing is facing up to the fact that some of the things that you've wanted to do don't fit. To try to put too much into the suitcase. The old image of the novel being a suitcase is a good one. William Faulkner once said,

'Cut all your beauties.' In other words, the passages where you've indulged yourself in things that you really like but you know in the back of your mind are not fitting into the novel. They may fit into another one.

By the time you're in the middle of the novel you've got the really hard work going on. That's where the threads have to tighten. Sometimes they'll sag, and if they sag you're in deep trouble. The novels that don't work for me are those where in the middle I suddenly feel he or she's lost it. But if in the middle the novel is still pulling you on and you know there's logic behind things, then you've got a good novel.

To quote Kenneth Slessor, 'Writing is a pleasure from hell.' Well, the end of a novel is a pleasure from hell. If it's a good novel the end will drag you along and it can mean, in my case anyway, work that sometimes goes for nine-hour days, which is a bit insane. You should never write for that long, as a rule. But if a novel forces you to do that at the end, it's a good sign.

———

I think a novel is a piece of architecture. A lot of my family were architects and maybe that influenced me. I think that if you don't get the ground plan right, then the whole building might not work, so I spend as long as six months simply making notes before I write a word. I must have the plans in some sort of shape. I must know what I'm doing and I find it's easier to do that by making notes. And that's longhand, since I come from the age of the fountain pen, and only then will I go on to the word processor. That doesn't mean that the novel will follow those plans exactly; sometimes it will diverge hugely, but at least if you have the plan, you think you know where you're going. And even if it does diverge, then there'll be a logic in that.

———

I find personally that there is no room in your life for anything else but writing. I spent a lot of my life in the ABC and during the years I had a family and was working in the ABC I more or less stopped writing. At the age of forty I thought, If I don't get out of this I won't write again, so I quit and went back to Tasmania and lived from hand to mouth. From that day to this I've never done an honest job of work again and I never have any problem writing. You can't come home from a demanding job and sit down and write. There are superhuman people who do it, or try to do it, but normal writing is a full-time occupation.

———

Writers should be truthful to the theme they've taken and not betray it. That is, don't twist it for the market or for anything else, but write truthfully. At the same time, think of the person reading it, and think of trying to interest them.

dorothy dunnett

Dorothy Dunnett was born in 1923 in Dunfermline, Scotland. She has published a total of twenty-three books, including two major series of historical novels, *The Lymond Chronicles* – of which her first novel, *The Game of Kings*, was a part – and *The House of Niccolo*. Her other titles include *King Hereafter* and a series of detective novels. In 1992 she was awarded an OBE for services to literature. She lives in Edinburgh.

Eachmarcach looked at the hostages. Two were elderly. One was a raw-faced youth of fifteen with an unpleated shock of fair hair, playing some sort of game in the dust. None of the captives was shackled, and the guard stood about, watching. The youth talked and laughed all the time. He had a laugh like the flapping of crows' wings. For the son of a famous beauty, he was, as usually happens, nothing out of the way. Eachmarcach said, 'That's how to live to be eighty. Don't trust yourself into English hands without first asking for English hostages, Alfgar. That's what the boy's called. Alfgar, the sole heir to Mercia.'

From *King Hereafter*

I'm a portrait painter – I'm not a writer at all. I'm a very bad example for people who write all through college and read everything and practise and go to writers' circles. I was in the civil service. In my mid-thirties I ran out of the kind of historical novel that I like to read. My husband's a newspaper editor, and newspaper editors just tell people to go and do things, even their wives. And he said, 'Why not write your own, and while you're at it, make it into a series because people like series.'

So as an obedient wife I thought, All right. I picked this period when Mary Queen of Scots was very small, only four years old. I realised why nobody else had written about this period, because it was very bad to research.

It was the first book I'd ever written in my life. My American editor phoned up after the second or third book and said, 'Dorothy, how many books are there going to be in this series?', which meant that I had to get down to slicing up the history and the story. I said, 'I think it's going to be six.' So that let him do his budgeting, which I hadn't really thought of at the time.

I've written two series of historical novels and each of them has a central fictitious hero. The first of them was in very classical heroic mould – you know, the kind of King Arthur, Charlemagne, Mel Gibson, the lot – whom everyone fell in love with, including me. That was six books, and by the time the sixth book was coming out I got sixteen-page letters from people saying, 'If you kill him I can't go on living,' which makes you think twice as an author, actually.

I'm just about to publish the last of another series of

eight books. Same idea, a very strong central character, but this time I've been doing my best to get away from the romantic hero. The guy starts as an apprentice in a dye yard in Bruges in the fifteenth century. He has a flair for numbers and can therefore hope to become a trader and a banker and explorer and move all over the world, but he is unprepossessing physically. That's very difficult to put across, because readers really want a romantic hero. I'm going to make them like this guy regardless, for his mind, his wit and for other qualities he has. It sort of worked, I think.

———

There are many historical writers who write series, and in all of these there is a fictitious central figure, but he grows and matures a bit from book to book – a chap who's a cabin boy in book one is an admiral by book whatever. But there isn't an overall story, or only a very big one. There'll be perhaps a love affair and a wife and a separation, but there isn't a plot that runs all the way through. I decided I liked Hornblower very much – when my husband Alistair said a series, that's what came to mind. Then I thought I might as well make it cohesive and have an overall plan.

Each book had its own plot, its own mystery – where the reader had a chance of deciding what the secret was, and you've left reasonable clues – and at the end I hoped they didn't get it but felt, Oh, I should have got it. So each book had that element – a series of mysteries which would arc right through and only be solved at the last one. I also wrote mainly in dialogue, without the authorial voice coming in very much, except to set a scene. It meant that readers had to interpret what was going on through the dialogue and through the description of the movements that the characters were making. If there's any description it has to be significant.

————

I've done a lot of judging of literary prizes, and you can always tell a tongue-in-the-cheek journalist who's decided to write the prize-getting book, because he or she is not in love with the leading character but has decided this is the character that's going to appeal – it's all put in artificially.

You need to empathise, even if you are treating somebody who hasn't got the full range of lovable qualities; you have to have aspects of the nature of your hero or protagonist that tune in with your nature. Really, I think for technical reasons as much as anything else, you are not going to draw your reader through the story unless they like the central character, and if *you* don't particularly like them – well, you're up a gum tree.

————

I think that making research invisible comes with experience. Probably the first one or two books that I wrote were full of everything. You think you're never going to publish everything else. Of course in my case, my first novel is still in print after forty years because it's the key one. But as time has gone on, I perhaps have learned to get wiser. As far as the history is concerned, you learn it's difficult because you come across wonderful fresh stuff you'd like to use and it's going to pull it out of shape.

————

I write too quickly because I have to publish every two years. When you're writing a series, if you let it go for more than two years between books, readers can get bored. They expect a book every two years. The books take about fourteen months to write and then there's all the copyediting and so on that goes after. So the result is the actual writing is very fast. It's a chapter every two days, with about two days to do all the research leading up to each chapter.

Occasionally there will be a block of history that gets in because at that point I'm thinking, I'm not sure if I'm going to get this in later on. I would say to anybody, anyway, if you're not writing a series, if you can afford the time to do it, finish the book, put it away, go and have a holiday, and then come back and look at it and you will know if there's too much history in it.

———

If you set a book in one particular era, or a series of books in one particular era, you must then decide whether to have modern English or whether you're going to have a kind of 'gadzookery'. There's a form of very simple archaic English that has been used very successfully by a number of authors going back to the sixteenth and seventeenth centuries. In my case I don't have any choice because my books are set all over Europe, when a really good trader was reckoned to speak fifteen or sixteen languages. In those days the Romance languages – all the languages based on Latin – were not so different, so it was possible for a merchant to move and pick up the language and even to pick up Turkish and Arabic. If you have a hero who is speaking English and periodically dropping into French, for example, you can rearrange the wording of the sentence in a French style although you're still using English, just to remind people that this is not English the fellow's speaking.

So it is a kind of neutral modern English which equates to the emotion or the feeling or the tone of what is actually going on. And to remind people that characters are not actually speaking modern English, I use a lot of quotations from poetry and from music and from prose text, letters and that kind of thing, and that is always inserted in its original language, which annoys my copyeditor.

> *Joleta, her hair in viperish coils around her neck, one sleeve off, and her feet bare and quick as a goat's, was marked dusky red like a school boy where he had sent furniture flying, and where Lymond's steely fingers, controlling by grip in lieu of breaking her bones, had discoloured the milky flesh. And all the time, her teeth set, she lunged from side to side, seizing what weapons she could. A pewter ale-mug hammered at his near shoulder and, wrenched away, was replaced by a sliver of glass, which slit both their hands before she dropped it. With windy sobbing, possessed by her fury, there was nothing she would not risk to defeat him, even to laying hands on his sword. For Lymond, that was the end. Holding her hard, he spoke sharply. 'Joleta. Don't be stupid. I'll have to hurt you.'*

> From *The Disorderly Knights*

The actual writing is bliss. It's wonderful devising the story, doing the research. I love the research. Then I sit down in front of the word processor. And of course novelists are all damaged people – we are all writing to escape, just as readers of fiction are reading to escape. I sit down and swan into this world of my own creating.

When I got to the end of the Lymond series, a very nice journalist from the London *Times* who'd been in touch with me all the way through phoned me up and said, 'Are you nearly finished?' And I said, 'I'm going to finish tomorrow.' And she said, 'How do you feel?' And I said, 'As if I'd dropped dead. It is terrible; after tomorrow I'm going to have nothing to think about.' She sent me a crate of spring flowers from London to Edinburgh on the overnight train. It's an addiction, it's dreadful.

———

I have to remember what I meant by everything. I never discuss what I'm writing with anybody while I'm writing it, or before I'm writing it, and therefore I've had no reaction to anything until the manuscript actually goes into the hands of my editor. So the first days with the editor are wonderful, because I'm getting the very first reaction to all of my work for the last fourteen months.

I have two editors, one in New York, Bob Gottlieb, and in London, Richenda Todd. Bob will take his time. I'm waiting for his phone call and then he will ring up from Miami or from his flat in Paris and say, 'Dorothy, I loved it! There are just two or three little things . . .' I'm thinking, Great. But the lovely thing he does is that he asks me to write new scenes, which is the nicest thing you can do for an author who's just finished a book. Everything's in your mind, you love your characters, and here is your editor saying, 'I would have liked to have seen a confrontational scene. You just mention it, you don't show it. There are just a few pages.' And it's lovely. I sit down and I write the whole scene that evening and I fax it off.

Sometimes it's sixteen pages of, 'You've got "really" in two sentences here . . .' When you write at the speed I do, this is when they're picking up everything. Occasionally I had a chap who lost his virginity in two different books and that was really difficult. And now and then I feel there are things I should go back and rework more carefully. On the whole, I am just filled with awe at the things people can pick up for me and I'm endlessly grateful. It's very hard work.

————

I have to provide all the material for the maps, of which there are several in each book. This is the author's responsibility. And in my case I'll be covering huge areas of Europe in the fifteenth or the sixteenth century, when the rivers and the towns all had different names. I have a sweet cartographer called Peter McClure who phones me up and says, 'Dorothy, there isn't room to have both names of Dubrovnik.' When you think about the size of a map and an ordinary sort of book, it reduces very small. Then of course my readers like to go to all these places, and they meet one another and they go off on tours to Bruges or whatever, and they like to be able to see routes. So there's all that.

There is the list of characters – 130 historical characters

in the present series, and thirty fictitious ones. When you identify historical characters, you then have to find out what the relationships between them are. It's like the appendix in an historical dictionary, which means a tremendous amount of research before I actually type all that stuff out, and you have to identify who is whose half-stepbrother by a marriage to somebody else, which you have pushed aside to that moment. I'll do that at the end of the book. That can take a fortnight to do on its own.

———

There are people who like performing, like going round, and find it no problem, and that's a great help to the publisher because it means the readers can get in touch with an actual person. But by far the majority of writers are not happy doing that. They don't want to.

I went through all the horrifying stages of being petrified meeting everybody and talking through dinner parties and having to speak, and I spent about ten years being absolutely shivering frightened. Once that's behind you then it's much easier, because you can just be yourself. And I love meeting people.

———

First and foremost, be interested in other people. The turn-off when you read books, often, is that the author is interested only in himself or herself and their own opinions. If you're going to create rounded characters, you have got to know an enormous amount of other people and try to understand them.

Second, read, read, read. Better than anything you can learn from a teacher is getting into your head what is necessary in the way of rhythm and the flow of language, and what is turgid or boring; where you have got to step away from stuff and leave it, where you have got to tell your story economically – and it's only by reading the really good people. Reading bad writers is good too, it does a lot for your ego.

My own theory, having started in my mid-thirties, is that you can write a wonderful novel about your own experience in your teens and early twenties, but when you get beyond that, if you want to have anything with any scope or breadth, you really need to be in your thirties or coming up to forties. At some point somebody ought to tell you, 'Stop right now, just stop.' But there's a period in the middle which I think maybe gives hope to everybody else. Have your life, have your career, and start writing after that if you want to.

isobelle carmody

Isobelle Carmody was born in Wangaratta, Victoria in 1958. Her books include *The Obernewtyn Chronicles* and *Legendsong* series, *Green Monkey Dreams* and *Greylands*. She was joint winner of the Children's Peace Literature Prize in 1993 for *The Gathering*, and has won many other awards in the field of children's and young adults' literature. She lives in Victoria.

Did you bite someone? Jack enquired.

'I laughed at people, which is much worse. My laughter has sharper teeth than any dog. It tears people apart who wish to be taken seriously, but I could not help myself. There were many complaints and finally a man in a brown suit came and looked at me. He was very important and not use to being laughed at, but I could see he had dandruff on his collar, and there was a spot of his breakfast egg on his lapel. You should have seen him – so puffed up and proud of himself. I couldn't help but laugh and that made people see him as I did, and so they laughed too. All of a sudden everyone realised that for all his status in official matters, he was a man who lived alone and loveless. Anyone he lived with would

*have told him in a friendly fashion about those little imperfections.
It was clear to them all that he was hopelessly lonely and had no
one to love him, that he had no life other than in his official capacity as an inspector. Pity for him made me laugh. I laughed and
laughed and the audience was ravaged was by it. The ringmaster
said it was the final straw and so they exiled me from the circus
and brought me here.'*

From *Greylands*

I used to tell stories to my seven younger brothers and sisters.
I had to control them because I was left alone to look after
them, and the best way to do that was to scare them into submission, so I used to tell them horror stories. I think I learned
a very strong sense of audience control, and of liking audience control. I liked the sense that I could do what I wanted
with them, that they were a captive audience and that I could
make them feel whatever I wanted, depending on how well I
told my story.

I also used to have them act out parts of the story, which I
would make up as we went along. I'd say, 'Okay, we're all running away from an orphanage.' When I was a kid, almost all of
my stories began with everybody running away from an orphanage. I used to begin with us in an orphanage because I hated my
mum, so I used to kill her off in every book or story I wrote.

I don't think it is actually very unusual for kids to write
books. I think every second kid has written a book. Maybe
it's *Mr Fly's Adventures*, but it's a full book, and sometimes it's
twenty or thirty pages from a kid who almost writes nothing,
and may do very badly at school.

The thing is, that love of telling a story is very strong, and it can be absolutely killed. You have to be very careful about not killing the spark that's actually making a kid want to tell a story in the first place. For me, the only difference is that I kept rewriting and rewriting, and each time I rewrote I got a little better than the time before, and not just because I was rewriting but because I was elaborating and reconsidering. Being a voracious reader, I was seeing that other people did this better, or that there was a much better way to begin or to end, or how to handle a certain situation, and I was constantly being enriched by all of that. So the book [*Obernewtyn*] grew and grew from the shape that it had been when I was fourteen, and it kept going until I was about twenty-one.

I didn't send it off in all those years because I didn't think it was good enough. It wasn't as good as the books I was reading in the library. I didn't show it to anyone, I just could tell that myself. Any kid can tell this is a better book than that – what's good storytelling and what's bad storytelling. In every class there's a kid who's a good storyteller and everybody will stop to listen to him or her talk. Good writers are like that; they just have a knack of being able to tell a good story.

———

I set out to write a connected series. I didn't write one and then think, That was good, I'll do another one like *Rambo Fifteen*. I didn't decide, based on the response of the market to the books, to write them. When you write a series, and it's connected from the start and you know the beginning and the end, then there's a reason for doing it. It's not just spinning out a series, it's just a lovely big canvas to work on. It enables you to take big gaps of time to think in between each section of the series, and it allows you to explore things in a longer form. It allowed me to grow as I was writing the series. I think you can really see the character of Elspeth, who in some ways I guess is me, growing through the series. I was in my teens when I wrote *Obernewtyn*, in my twenties when I wrote *The Far Seekers*, in my thirties when I wrote *Ashling*, and I've only just published *The Keeping Place*, which is the fourth one. God knows, I might be in my fifties by the time I do the fifth and final one.

———

Fantasy is a category that's applied externally, it's certainly not one I applied to myself. I didn't even know there was a category with that name when I was growing up. There were no fantasy books in my school library. There were the Narnia books – *The Lion, the Witch and the Wardrobe*. I loved those books, so I sought more like that, and there was some science fiction which was interesting as well, so I pursued my interest that way.

When I began to write, naturally I wrote in the form that I liked. For me, fantasy was a way of stepping back from the real world in order to think about the real world. Once upon a time, what was called fantasy would have been called myth, and would have been honoured in a way that fantasy is not honoured. Some fantasy deserves not to be honoured, but the kind that I write, and the kind that I like, deals with real issues. It's basically looking at the real world through a refracted mirror, so I really see it as a very philosophical medium.

It's a big mistake for people who want to write fantasy to think, Oh, I'm writing fantasy. Because you begin to immediately see certain boundaries to what you can write. It's much better not to have that approach. It's a better book, it has more integrity in its own self, if you don't do that. One of the other mistakes people who write fantasy make is that they focus on the world-building – this elaborate world with elaborate characters and elaborate rules and laws, and they forget the most important thing of all, which is characterisation. There's no way to enter a science fiction or fantasy novel without going through the door of a character, and that character has to be real.

———

A book comes in a couple of parts. First of all, for me, you have an intellectual idea. For instance, you would want to write about friendship or the demands of friendship. Then you think about that a lot, you notice things in the world, you see bits in the newspapers and on television, people talk, and anything around that topic interests you. It's like a piece of sticky flypaper – that's what your head should be like. Bits stick to it, and after a while you have quite a lot of material, but it isn't focused in any way. Then one day a character will appear.

Every character is *you* ultimately, the bad and the good all has to rise from you. If you produce an evil character that you can't trace back to some seed of something you've done wrong, it doesn't even stand up as a character, unless you're deliberately creating a kind of a cardboard character. But if you want it to live as a real character, you have to delve into yourself. Therefore no character should be purely evil, no character should be purely good. Looking at monsters and angels, you're just exploring the extremities of human character anyway, it's just pushing it one step further.

> *Merlin was surprised to find she missed the scatterling youth.*
>
> *He had treated her well, though she had hardly been appreciative at the time. He was the only one since she had wakened to have offered her unconditional friendship. She had not spoken to a friend since . . . she couldn't remember when. She laughed bleakly at her own joke.*
>
> *She had failed to see Ford's value because she had been too preoccupied with her own problems. The truth was, she thought sadly, she had been more than slightly frightened by his savage appearance – his scarred eye and his near nakedness. She was ashamed of her prejudices, but in honesty, she had to admit that she had been even more unnerved by his sudden interest in her. Remembering the hungry way he had looked at her, she shivered.*
>
> From *Scatterlings*

You can have an incredibly detailed map which tells you the names of every building, the dimensions of it, and where the trees are, but it still won't tell you what it feels like to walk along that road on a particular day, what thoughts will go through your mind, what people you'll see and what will happen to you. To my mind, it's much better to keep it in your head rather than write it down. My idea of planning is just to think a lot about what you're writing, and if you possibly can to talk a lot about it to people, because it should obsess you to that extent. You should bore the hell out of everybody with your ideas and listen to what they have to say. So I'm not in favour of writing a plan, except the most basic sort of notes. A plan, to my mind, should always be very short, very simple and very basic. The more basic, the better. And the rougher, the better.

When young writers ask me for advice, that would always be what I would say: Write as fast as you can. Don't worry about wonderful adjectives, don't worry about beautiful sentence construction; in fact, don't even worry about your grammar. Just get it all down. If it takes you two years to write it down, then it should be longer than that before you finish it. You need to rework and rework and rework, because when you first finish a draft, you can't possibly imagine that you've even explored your own idea very fully. Editing is not correcting the spelling and making the writing look neater, it's really going into the characters.

That long process of editing is always a process of cutting and cutting back to nothing, and then elaborating, and then cutting back to nothing and then elaborating. It sounds counterproductive in a way, but if you write a scene and then cut back all the unnecessary words, it leaves you the space to really focus on the things that might be more important.

———

In a story, dialogue shouldn't be there to tell you what one person says to another – that's the most simplistic approach to dialogue. Dialogue should be there to build character, so if a piece of dialogue doesn't tell you something about a character, well, what's the point of it? You can in two seconds flat write a sentence which précis a conversation, so you don't actually need all of those words. The reason for spinning it out in direct speech is to actually have a more vivid sense of a character.

———

I don't sit and wait for inspiration to strike. You'd never start if that's what you did. Inspiration happens while you are working. Some days I sit down and I feel very uninspired and I work, and at the end of the day I may have stumbled on inspiration and got terribly excited five minutes after I began or one hundred minutes after I began, or it may not come at all. The important thing is to keep writing. If you stop and start, of course you're going to come to a writer's block. I'm not sure I believe in it really, I think it's a posturing that takes over and gets in the way – better not to think of writer's block at all.

———

The book goes to the publisher when I'm finished with it, and then there'll be some work with an editor. Sometimes it goes to a reader. If I'm in dispute with an editor over a section, they might send it off to a reader to find out what that reader's impression is. We did this with one of my novels at some point because the editor and I came to a major dispute over something in the book.

Then after that the book will be galley-proofed. The pages come back to you exactly as they'll be in the book but without a cover, and then sometimes a writer can rewrite from that point. I did once in a book – rewrote a final section and added 200 pages, much to the publisher's horror – but the general principal is that it's almost finished. You go through and you correct, the galley proofs are corrected, the thing is printed. You have some say in the cover, or no say, depending on where you are in your career and how big the publisher is, and after that the book begins to have a life of its own.

———

The minute you begin to think about a book, and you mention it to your publishers, suddenly publicity people are talking about it as if it's a real thing, and people will be asking, 'So when are you going to finish that?' You feel the breathing down the back of your neck. When the book's actually printed and distributed, that's when you're required to go out and publicise it. You may do interviews, or you may decide to go and speak at schools, talk on the radio, and read excerpts from it.

It's a strange business, because there's no telling that a person who writes brilliantly will be able to speak and sell their books. That's much more of a requirement in the world now than it used to be before. You'd like to think that you could just write your book and the fairies would take it away and people would receive it, but that process has to happen, that commercial process.

———

Sending your short stories to competitions is a really good way to have your work out there. That's because the judges of those competitions are often the editors from publishers. A friend of mine sent in a huge novel to the Vogels and didn't get anywhere because 'it wasn't very good' – her words, not mine. But nevertheless, someone on the panel was from a publisher and approached her later on and said, 'What would you think about writing a detective novel for us?' She's written about fifteen of them now.

———

Writing is the best thing in the world to do. People often think you sit in a room doing nothing except write. Well, I'm not in the room there writing – I'm off on a quest in a boat with a sword in my hand. I live probably the best life that anybody could ever live. I recommend it as a career option absolutely.

But if you're going into it because you think you'll make money, or you think you'll be famous, forget about it, it's just not worth it. You might as well go and make money in some ordinary job, because you'll make more ultimately. You have to love it, and you have to love it so that you would do it no matter what. They're the only ones that will last long enough through all the rewrites and all the stuff that comes in between to make it right through to the end. You have to have an absolute passion for it.

jennifer johnston

Jennifer Johnston was born in Dublin in 1930 and has written numerous novels and plays. She won the 1979 Whitbread Prize for *The Old Jest*, the *Evening Standard* Best First Novel Award for *The Captains and the Kings*, and the *Yorkshire Post* Best Book of the Year twice, for *The Captains and the Kings* and for *How Many Miles to Babylon?* She was also shortlisted for the *Daily Express* Best Book of the Year in 1992 for *The Invisible Worm*, and for the Booker Prize in 1977 for *Shadows on Our Skin*. Her other novels include *The Railway Station Man*, *Fool's Sanctuary*, *Two Moons* and *The Gingerbread Woman*. She now lives in Derry.

Joe listened until he could no longer hear the sound of their feet and the mutter of their voices going up the hill, then angrily he began to rattle out the stove. He carried the ashes out into the back yard and tipped them into the dustbin. A bright cold moon grinned in the polished evening blue of the sky. The smell of the gas works blew on the air. Ash puffed up from the bin, choking his nose. He stood still with the ash pan in his hand listening to the sounds of people living that somehow you never seemed aware of

*in the day-time. A baby crying, the clatter of cups, the rise and fall
of television voices, laughter, the creak of a door, each sound quite
clear and individual, and of course, but now far away, the
inevitable ambulance. The walls between the houses would be silver soon under the moon and frost would sparkle on the roofs.*

From *Shadows on our Skin*

I didn't start writing until I was in my mid-thirties, and I had
to find out whether I was able to do it or not. That really took
me several books before I had the confidence to realise that
this was not just a flash in the pan, that it was actually something I could do. I had to work out disciplines for myself,
because I think I started off with the notion in my head, like
so many other people have, that you wait for inspiration to
come. Of course that is a very spurious notion. You don't wait
for inspiration to come – you have to sit down and work, and
that is what inspiration is, in a way.

The first couple of years when I was writing, I was never
finishing anything. I was writing and rereading it and being
very unsatisfied with what I was doing and tearing it up and
throwing it away. I wrote about two novels that I never finished, then a voice came into my head and said, 'Just finish
this one.' Maybe you think it's awful – stop looking back at it,
keep going on, keep going on until you put that last full stop.

I learned then that it's not until that last full stop is there
that you've got anything to look back at, because you don't
understand the pattern of the writing, you don't understand
the rhythms in which you're telling this story until it's finished. That was the first very serious lesson that I found – that

to finish something is actually the most important thing you can do, and not to look at it seriously until then. You can make tiny little adjustments if you want to, but don't torture yourself with saying, 'No, that won't do!' Because in fact, when you take the whole, that may do very well.

———

An enormous amount of my writing comes out of my head without me apparently knowing why when I'm writing it. I start off with my main character and a little germ of a plot. I very much feel this person wants to speak, this person wants to be released from a prison of some sort, and I have the key. I just sort of stagger along from there and I get a little confidence, and I see what this person has on their mind, what their problem is, what their secret is. Writing is to a large degree about secrets, and a lot of these secrets are things that you find inside yourself.

———

I have never been able to structure a book formally before I sit down to write it. Unless I'm sitting in front of my word processor, nothing happens. I don't particularly like writing. I don't enjoy the process of writing. There are wonderful moments of great excitement when you suddenly find a river flowing out of yourself – of ideas, words – and they're all fitting in together neatly. This happens very, very seldom and when it does you feel at the end of that day, Oh that was absolutely wonderful! I have enjoyed that day! But then sometimes you go back and you look at that piece, and you cross it out.

An awful lot of the time the words come out so slowly, like the treacle in *Alice in Wonderland*, and that can be quite depressing. And yet you know you have to go on. There is no way that I can stop now once I get past about page twenty. I have to go on. It's very slow because I don't really go back and rewrite very much. I will go back and I will cut bits out. I will go back and I will change infelicities of language, but what comes out of the treacle tends to be 95 per cent finished product. I keep saying to myself, I think you're doing this all wrong, really. But I can't seem to do it any other way.

————

When I started writing first, I was very specifically writing about Ireland, and at the stage when I was starting to be published, the troubles in the north had started. So I became very obsessed with this thing of violence and war and waste, and the nature of what was causing us to hate each other in Ireland. The main characters were men and they were damaged by their own personal pasts and by their family backgrounds, and that's something I really do find absolutely fascinating. People talk about dysfunctional families – I have actually never come across a functional family, so I find it quite interesting to write about why we're dysfunctional, and not necessarily the reasons why people think we ought to be dysfunctional. Those are the themes really. It's the dysfunctionality of human beings and the power of friendship, which can be sublime.

Friendship is a much more interesting notion to me than the interest of love, unless you're talking about love in a religious way, which is something totally different. But the notion of love that we all have in our heads – you grow up, you fall in love with somebody, you get married, you go on loving them forever – I find that that is something I really like to take the lid off, because I think it's a fairy story that we have to disabuse people of. People think it will be terribly easy once you find that thing called love, and all your problems are going to be solved – even sophisticated young people tend to have this notion in their heads – but the notion of loyalty and friendship to me is much more interesting.

> *They danced in silence. After a while she raised the hand that had been holding his empty shoulder and touched the destroyed face.*
>
> *She thought it was going to alarm her, the feel of the dry cobbled skin, but to her fingers' surprise it was almost like running them over a canvas, grainy stretched parts and then densely textured paint, but warm like flesh should be, not canvas-cool.*
>
> *The music stopped. The needle whirled and no sound came any longer to them as they stood close together in the middle of the room, her fingers gently touching his face.*
>
> *'Please,' he said suddenly to her. 'Please, oh Helen, please.'*
>
> From *The Railway Station Man*

One of the reasons I don't like my first book (and I'm not mad about the second one either) is that I had a lot of characters who were just furniture. I had to teach myself how to make even the smallest characters real – like Chekhov plays, even the servant who comes in with the bowl of soup is a real person. It's terribly easy just to have people as props. It's a very difficult thing to explain to people who are writing that if you're going to be a serious writer you've got to teach yourself how to make a character breathe, how to make a character appear to have a life even when you turn the page over and they're not there any longer. I can't explain how it is that that happens, I just know that it's one of the differences between good writing and just storytelling.

One of the other things that is very important is to understand about the texture of writing. Writing is not just putting words down on the page, it is also to do with that thing hideously entitled the subtext, which comes out of your subconscious. I sometimes find myself writing a paragraph or even just a sentence and wondering why have I just written it. I won't know why until I finish the book and I go back, and I will see that it is not necessarily a bridging sentence but it's a sentence that is connected in some way to something that's gone before, or in some way with something that's going to come later on, and it adds to the texture of the book.

––––––

Writing dialogue is to do with listening very carefully to the rhythms of people's speech. Maybe this is something to do with the fact that I was brought up in the theatre and my father was a writer of plays and my mother was an actress. When you write dialogue in a novel, you write the sort of dialogue that people think they speak, but not actually the dialogue they do speak. These are the words we like to think we say, and people recognise it and say, 'Your dialogue is wonderful,' but in fact nobody really talks like that at all. If you examine my books very carefully there would be little bits of dialogue that are quite good, very short, but by and large, when people launch into long conversations and you inspect that, it is purely literary dialogue.

————

I think the hardest thing, and the thing you have to work hardest at, is truth. It doesn't matter what your story's about. It doesn't matter in a way who your protagonists are, but you have to make it true. I don't just mean technically true, but I mean your reader has to be able to trust you. So you can't be playing games with them, you have to actually give them the truth that you know, and sometimes this is just a painful thing to do.

————

Read, read, read and read, everything you can lay your hands on. I don't know who it was, but there was some famous writer who said, 'Apply the seat of the pants to the seat of chair,' and that's about the best thing that you could do. Don't believe for one single second that some sort of genius comes and taps you on the shoulder. It is just hard work, and you've got to realise that right from the word go.

luke davies

Luke Davies was born in Sydney in 1962 and has worked as a teacher, journalist and script editor. He has written four collections of poetry, including *Running with Light*, and two novels, *Candy* and *Isabelle the Navigator*.

There were good times and bad times, but in the beginning there were more good times. When I first met Candy: those were like the days of juice, when everything was bountiful. Only much later did it all start to seem like sugar and blood, blood and sugar, the endless dark heat. But I guess the truth is, it didn't really take all that long for things to settle into a downward direction. It's like there's a mystical connection between heroin and bad luck, with some kind of built-in momentum factor. It's like you're cruising along in a beautiful car on a pleasant country road with the breeze in your hair and the smell of eucalypts all around you. The horizon is always up there ahead, unfolding towards you, and at first you don't notice the gradual descent, or the way the atmosphere thickens. Bit by bit the gradient gets steeper, and before you realise you have no brakes, you're going pretty fucking fast.

So what did we do, once the descent began? We learned how to drive well, under hazardous conditions. We had each other to egg each other on. There was neither room nor need for passengers. Maybe also we were thinking that one day our car would sprout wings and fly. I saw that happen in Chitty Chitty Bang Bang. *It's good to live in hope.*

From *Candy*

I was always writing, I grew up in a house full of books. I was writing silly poems and things at seven, eight years old, but at the age of thirteen I discovered this incredible world of books. Actually the book that changed it all was *Cannery Row* by John Steinbeck. It was the moment when I realised that I was not reading the set class novel that they'd given me in Year Seven and that I'd found something else that belonged to another world.

So at the age of thirteen the most important thing to me was poetry. I discovered the world of adult poetry and that was my obsession. It was a long, slow apprenticeship. Maybe by the time I was twenty I was beginning to write a poem now and then that resembled something that had promise, but I'm certainly glad that's where my obsession was for many years before I started writing prose.

———

Ultimately, I believe if somebody wants to be a good writer, what they need to do is read a lot. You'll generally find that people who are obsessed with reading may have it in them to also become good writers. There are creative writing courses out there that can probably help to develop and hone some skills, but I don't think they can turn a non-writer into a good writer. I think ultimately that skill comes from an awareness of other things that are going on – lots of reading, persistence and practice.

———

Inspiration often comes as an unexpected thing, and after the arrival of inspiration I've often set up the project that I'm working on. I like to live my life with an attitude of openness to the arrival of things, an intense curiosity about things, and the greater that curiosity, maybe the more that inspiration can arrive. But if I look at my work, and I look at the percentage of inspiration versus the actual work, the inspiration is tiny fragments of that time line.

———

I think it's very healthy to have purpose, a sense of where you want to go, but then letting go of the results, not clinging to *this* must happen, *this* must be where I go, because once you put something into action, I think the real beauty is when you're then taken somewhere where you weren't expecting to go. On a very concrete level I think perseverance is important, a kind of blind faith in oneself, in the face of many rejections. I think the Buddha said impatience is the only sin. I think there's some validity to that.

———

I have discovered that it is absolute death to my writing if I am to ever think, too much, about the sense of a market out there. In a very old-fashioned and corny way, I absolutely believe in the unshakability of being true to the integrity of your own directions and letting the rest of the stuff work itself out. If I start to write with a market in mind, then I can expect the inevitable hollowness to begin to enter into my work. I also feel fortunate that people like what I write. I'm not blind to the existence of a market, and I know things that I love and I know things that sell, but I think a heightened consciousness of how a market relates to my actual process of writing is an unhealthy place to be.

———

Candy is a book that is known to have certain vaguely semi-autobiographical elements in it – very vaguely, I should add, too. It's ultimately a novel, and arises out of things I knew, or things I knew of, or things I knew could happen, and so on. My next novel, *Isabelle*, I did do some research for. There's an important scene that takes place in a volcano, and I spent quite a lot of time on the Net and in encyclopaedias getting the technical details right. I tracked down a vulcanologist in Hawaii who very kindly read my chapter in exchange for a mere acknowledgement in the book and a signed copy when it came out.

And I went to Western Australia because I had the heroine of the book falling in love with a fisherman on the cray boats off the West Australian coast and I clearly knew that I needed to get the geography right, and I needed to get the deck life right. So some of that went into the book, but a lot of the research that I did didn't end up in the book, it didn't become important – a whole lot of stuff about marine navigation. The book ended up changing directions and it's not there now.

> *On the summit the day will turn black with the ash of your weight. Then* puff!*, you are gone, the lightest of birds, so insubstantial now that your wing cannot singe even cumulus clouds. The mobile mantle rises and partially melts. In the sulphide-rich torpor we sleep. Therefore the flight shall perish from the swift and the strong shall not strengthen his force, neither shall the mighty deliver himself. The excess heat of the magma can partially melt the host rock through which it ascends. He that is swift of foot shall not deliver himself; neither shall he that rideth the horse deliver himself. Heat lowers the density of the rocks and therefore the speed of the seismic waves that travel through them. But he that is courageous among the mighty shall flee away naked in that day. And the mountains shall drop sweet wine, and all the hills shall melt. All this will be yours. For an instant.*
>
> From *Isabelle the Navigator*

As a writer, I'm certainly very comfortable in the first person. Possibly that's because in a sense I'm still on my L-plates. I'm only up to my second novel, and maybe third-person point of view is more difficult to master and to manage. Maybe I will head in that direction and maybe I will always return to the first person. My next novel is a first-person narrative told through a woman's point of view, so there's a whole different set of issues going on there.

Strangely enough, we're in an era where this is an issue. It was certainly never considered to be an issue in the nineteenth century – male novelists with female protagonists, female novelists with male protagonists – and it's less of an issue when female writers write through the eyes of a male protagonist. But I keep getting people saying, 'Whoa, good luck to you, you're trying to write through a female's eyes.' It makes me nervous. I could get it wrong.

I think that's what it's all about. There are various degrees of boundary pushing, and it's nice to be out there pushing them. It keeps the sense of what it means to be a writer, and what it is that you're creating, alive.

———

I am one of these writers who had a very fortunate first-novel experience with the collaborative process of working with an editor. I was very open to outsiders' opinions, the opinions of people I trusted. In other words, I had a connection with an editor, and when they started to make criticisms, instead of getting egotistical and defensive, I tried to move outside of myself and see the truth in what they were saying. And strangely enough, I moved into this mode of thinking quite easily, and ultimately was very thankful for this collaborative situation.

Candy is a better novel because, after the first draft, at the point when I sold it to the publisher, the suggestions that were made about its shortcomings made sense to me, and I went away and started to work on finding solutions to these shortcomings. I probably would not have managed to see these things left to my own devices.

———

I think that all great literature is literature in which the author's ability to feel compassion with the story, with the characters that he's creating, creates warmth in the story. When stories are compassionless, when they don't contain that sense of sympathy for the vagaries of life and the suffering of the characters – those stories are the cold stories that I'm not interested in reading.

The word compassion comes from the Latin root *compassio*, which is 'with suffering'. In the really great books, we move through these emotional states and we suffer with the characters as they change. I love redemptive endings. A movie like *Breaking the Waves* is a movie that divides opinions. To me it's one of the great movies of many years and I absolutely love its almost cornily redemptive ending. There's a sense in *Candy* in which there's an ambiguously redemptive ending – there are uncertainties going on there about what actually happens to these two characters, but there is a kind of resolution in that direction.

———

I have a very obsessive mind. I can float around for days with these internal films running that involve the characters, or these ways of thinking through their minds, and so on. And I also think that sleep is really important and dreaming is really important. A lot of sleep is important because the good dreams that can help you through the fiction-writing process don't tend to come if you've only had five or six or seven hours' sleep. But eight or nine – ten now and again, I love a good ten now and again – can bring things into your subconsciousness and near the surface that relate to your characters.

I'm a night person. I can work easily well into the night until 4am and then have the big sleep. I'm working on trying to change these habits. I think to myself, I wonder what it would be like to go for a jog on the beach at 6.30am and begin the day from there? Instead I get up at nine and take my time and have breakfast and read the paper.

———

I love a good interior monologue. I think it's necessary to have a good ear. Again this question of openness comes up – the open ear, the open cerebral cortex – to sit on a bus and to be engaged with that rich beauty, even of the fragmentary kinds of language that we hear, the bits and pieces, the odd things. Real dialogue is strange. If you listen to real dialogue, it's very strange, and a lot of dialogue in novels is stilted, as if it's come from somewhere else, as if there's some literary parallel universe where people actually speak like that.

———

I think some level of social interaction is necessary. An isolated genius with a great manuscript in the countryside may be lucky and the genius of the manuscript may get recognised. But things can get lost in the great rush of the way the publishing world works. I think it's really helpful to have an agent, and of course the question remains that these days it's getting just as hard to get an agent to look at a manuscript as it is to get a publisher to look at one.

The agent's unsolicited piles can be just as big as the publisher's unsolicited manuscript piles. Nonetheless I'm sure there are ways, and mine happened by a set of circumstances, by getting a little name as a published poet, and that beginning to grow, and meeting people here and there – agents and publishers, and so on. If you're young you just have to take a deep breath and be a little bit pushy, and try to meet people at festivals and places like that, I suppose. It's an unfortunate truth, but it is a truth.

nicholas shakespeare

Nicholas Shakespeare was born in England in 1957. He grew up in Asia and South America and is the author of *The Vision of Elena Silves*, which won the Somerset Maugham Award, *The High Flyer* and *The Dancer Upstairs*. He has also written a biography of Bruce Chatwin.

Do you realize the horror of this? A woman used to movement, who is afraid of the dark, who is used to a lighted stage, now living in absolute darkness, no one to acknowledge her except the guard who collects the tray. There are no mirrors. She can't know what she looks like. Perhaps her eyes will milk up, like one of those deep-water, dark-dwelling fishes they net from the lake at that altitude.

She can't see what she's eating, what she's drinking, where she's defecating. She can have no idea whether it's night or day. How does she know when to sleep, when to wake? Dreams must be her only light, but what can she dream of, and how does she feel when she wakes from a dream and there's darkness and she knows she'll be waking to this room for the rest of her life, that until the grave this is what will greet her?

From *The Dancer Upstairs*

I've written three novels and I'm on my fourth, and in each case it's been like a pebble in the shoe. Suddenly somebody says a phrase or a scene and it's there, and you see it in total clarity for about a minute, and then you're condemned to two or three years of trying to retrace and recreate that clarity.

The genesis of *The Dancer Upstairs* is that I lived in Peru. I was obsessed by the leader of the Shining Path guerilla movement, who was a professor of philosophy, and he gave no interviews, he issued no manifestos. It was a very violent revolution, modelled on the Cambodian revolution. I'd lived in Cambodia in my childhood – I was now living in Peru. I was witnessing these murders taking place, I was witnessing the terror of a country. I was witnessing a movement that actually didn't explain what it was doing. The leaders were invisible, so of course I wanted to give a face to this man, and he was in hiding, so I created him in fiction in my first novel and then this came out in 1989. I'd created the fact that he had psoriasis as possibly one of the reasons that he would be in hiding. I wondered if there was an element of vanity to the fact he wouldn't be seen.

Two years after the novel came out, he was found by the police above a ballet studio in Lima, and I immediately had this image of a ballerina dancing below with mirrors, giving lessons to middle-class kids, while upstairs she was protecting this kind of fat revolutionary with curtained windows.

I saw the ballerinas in the shower afterwards, sweaty, naked, and the steam coming up through the floorboards on this man covered with sores, unable to look at the daylight, unable to look at himself (probably a mirrorless room), listening to the music of his favourite composers being kind of thumped repetitively by adolescent feet. That was an early image that I had.

> *From below he hears the squeak of shoes, a sound as of something sharply wrenched. He looks down to the rug. The squeaks mark the end of his reading. Downstairs they are beginning their exercises. For the next hour and a half the floor will become a sounding board for the thud, thud, thud of feet and the "one two three, one two three, one two three" of the teacher calling out the rhythm, and for the music, interrupted again and again, of his favourite composers.*
>
> From *The Dancer Upstairs*

The reason I was interested was that the policeman who discovered him above the ballet studio had gone through rubbish bags sifting, in a sense like a novelist, for anything – material to build up character – and he'd suspected this ballet studio, one of many, many buildings he'd suspected. So he was just casing this joint, and he'd go through the rubbish bags and he'd find psoriasis medicine and immediately he suspects that there's somebody living in the upstairs room. He does the raid and finds the leader of the world revolution upstairs.

Now, as soon as I heard this I knew what I wanted to do. I wanted to have the policeman, who himself, I discovered, was a philosopher (in a sense the policeman had been chasing Ezekiel, as I call him in the novel, for as long as I had been; I had been trying to recreate him in fiction since 1985, so I went to see the policeman and I told him that I already knew what I wanted to do), I wanted to have this honest policeman looking for the guerilla leader as the revolution encroaches on the city. Meanwhile he's got a daughter and he has rather a snobbish wife who wants her to have ballet lessons, so he saves all his overtime money and he pays for the ballet lessons in the studio and he begins to fall in love with the ballet mistress. So as the revolution is encroaching, he's getting more and more passionately in love with this woman, and finally the evidence is pointing to the district, and then to the street, and then to the house – and still he refuses to see that it's anything to do with the ballerina.

I wanted to have him capture the leader of the world revolution and save his country – in the same gesture bury his love and discover in that moment that this woman had been protecting the terrorist. I told the policeman this and he laughed, and I discovered a few days later that when he was young he'd been very much in love with a classical ballerina, to the extent that they were going to get married. It was she who said, 'I cannot marry you if you continue being a policeman. Could you not give this up?' And he thought for several days and said, 'No, it's my vocation.' So they had not married and they had not seen each other for twenty years. The policeman subsequently married and had children.

But the day after he captures Ezekiel, he gets a telephone call from the ballerina and she just tells him, 'You were right.' So this to me was confirmation, it's a validation of the fictional process, that you have a smell for a story, and often what you invent turns out to be very, very approximate to the truth. When I gave the policeman my first novel, in which I had Ezekiel suffering from psoriasis, he was again very amused at how accurately you can guess something.

———

I've only written one biography; I don't intend to write any others. I've written three novels. Fiction demands that you share a cigarette with your enemy, that you look him in the eye before you shoot, that you see him in all the roundness, that you don't judge him. I think that's very important. In a novel, if you judge your character it decays the character. I think you must be fascinated; in a sense you must be in love with them all, or you must be compassionate or at least empathetic with them all.

In my experience with the biography of Chatwin, who was a friend, who was somebody I greatly admired, I treated him in a ruthless light. In order to see through him and around him, I held him up to his own subjective light – very strong, cold light – in order to make him human too, because I think in both places you're after the truth, this nebulous quality.

Now, in fiction the truth is much easier to create, because you create it. If I tell you Ezekiel is feeling glum, you have no reason to doubt me. I mean you're not going to say, 'I think you're wrong, I think Ezekiel at this minute is incredibly happy.' If I tell you in nonfiction that Chatwin is feeling glum, how do we know? We don't know anything about anybody's life, let alone our own. Nonfiction is a very messy and imperfect science in trying to find out what happened, because you have to rely on testimonies. Eyewitnesses have their own reasons for telling you something, and everyone has an investment in remembering the past in a certain way. Each of them gives you a different interpretation of what went on, and the biographer has to sift through, prostrate himself before the options, and come up with some plausible, coherent narrative, and has to recognise – something that the novelist knows, the maxim of Nietzsche – that truth is a mobile army of metaphors. I think the biographer has to recognise that; the fiction writer knows that already. So they're very similar in many ways, but perhaps you have to be more ruthless in nonfiction with your characters.

There comes a moment in which somebody like Chatwin could degenerate into a kind of Daisy Bates figure, in which you're questioning everything they did and showing that it wasn't quite like that. But I don't think that's very interesting after a bit. I think the reader is quite generous. If you say to the reader, 'We don't know what went on, this is the best we can suspect went on,' I think the reader is then more on your side.

I think there was a biography of Sylvia Plath in which they tried to use the fictional muscle to dramatise what went on between Ted Hughes and Sylvia Plath when they first met. It loses all credibility, because you supply Ted Hughes and Sylvia Plath with emotions. How do you know they had them? You just don't trust that voice. No-one is interested, if you're writing a biography, in inventing something that did not happen. You're trying to find out what happened, and perhaps in trying to find out what happened you have to prostrate yourself before the options.

———

The painter Balthus tells a story of Francis Bacon, who abandons his history of the world after he discovers that a murder he observed from his window differs from the account of every other eyewitness.

The idea that we can resurrect the past in a way that all parties who participated in it will judge fair I think is a hopeless enterprise, because you're dealing with competing and conflicting subjectivities. You can have a literal truth, that Chatwin was wearing red trousers, but whether the truth is that Chatwin was behaving badly to his wife by telling her to go away outside a restaurant, or whether the fact is that she went away because the restaurant said, 'Sorry we can't have dogs' – the biographer has to make sense of all these interpretations, and recognise that there are motives invisible to the people who are telling you the story. The truth has its own smell eventually, and suddenly you know what went on in a certain way.

———

I began as a journalist, and journalism in a sense is acceptable cliché, in that you have to use short phrases. Writing, I discovered, is entirely the opposite. Every word has to be minted for that sentence. Vargas Llosa has a marvellous quotation from Flaubert – you're kind of spurning words the whole time, like the fathers of Sparta casting out children with crippled feet.

Vargas Llosa told me about having a card index which he had begun with *The City and the Dogs,* his first novel, and I asked him how it worked. So for my second novel I started doing this. I have a card for the way people look at each other or for the way people smile, and you build up this and you find it incredibly useful. You find a phrase in a book or a word you like, and you build up this card index. I don't think it's scientific or anti-inspiration, I think it's a very useful arsenal, and you mustn't depend on it too much but I think it keeps you on your feet.

Secondly, Bruce Chatwin gave me this advice – when you've finished your first draft of the novel, then do the synopsis and do it in prose and do it up to 10 000 words. In writing it out in prose, you suddenly see what you have to lose, what you have to put in. So it shows you what darlings to kill. Your first draft is like clay on the pedestal, but you know it's all there and you quite like it, but you can't see how to begin. The synopsis really is agony. You have to crush your entire experience of writing that first draft, filter it and crush it into these 10 000 words, and by the end of that process you know exactly what you've got to do.

Chatwin's other piece of advice to me was in a sense a kind of homage to Flaubert: 'If you want readers to feel emotion in your characters, don't beg them to feel emotion.' Chatwin's example was that you have this weeping mother and child – just describe them from the outside like a *tableau vivant*, the tears running down the face; just describe what's going on. Don't have any emotion and the reader will then feel it.

———

When I'm stuck, or when I'm in the saddle of a novel, at night before I go to bed I write a paragraph. The one criteria is it must be something that I've never admitted to myself, or that it must not be tasteful. It must be something that we think about all day without realising we think about it. I mustn't think about it, it must just come. I write during the day and at night before I go to bed I'll write this paragraph.

Now, what I discovered in this exercise is that you never know what you're going to find pornographic. (I mean it's not only sexual, in fact it ceases to be.) At its best, something incredible comes out very easily, and it comes out because you haven't thought about it. It has to come out in a sort of narrative form with its own rhythms.

I have found that these paragraphs are kind of like bushfire that you can bring into and light up sections of your book when you need to. I have found that it has really helped me in moments when I need energy. I've written something flat and it needs to be better, and I look back through this notebook and I bring out some phrase or some metaphor or some energy, and I pour it like gasoline on the page and it lights up. You have to rewrite it and you have to edit it, but something is injected.

―――――

Borges said to me, 'You must never look for beauty, you must let beauty come to you. Those who look for beauty are mere journalists.' At some level that has taken root. I think it's wrong to go out and look for a novel to write. I think you've got to wait for the pebble in your shoe, because you're going to have to give it so much that it's got to come from some-where interesting. It's got to have come from an area that you want answered, and the pebble in the shoe is an unmistakable feeling, and it's not pleasant, and once you've got it out you can walk again until you get a bit of gravel in next time.

thomas keneally

Thomas Keneally was born in Sydney in 1935. He studied for the priesthood and worked as a schoolteacher before publication of his first novel, *The Place at Whitton*, in 1964. He was nominated for the Booker Prize four times before being awarded it in 1982 for *Schindler's Ark*. He has written numerous other novels, including *The Chant of Jimmie Blacksmith, Towards Asmara, The Playmaker* and, most recently, *Bettany's Book*. He has won the Miles Franklin Award twice, in 1967 for *Bring Larks and Heroes* and in 1968 for *Three Cheers for the Paraclete*. He has also written nonfiction, most recently a history of Irish emigration, *The Great Shame*.

She was an orphan now. Her name was Lucy Rochester. Her sleeping brother was Hector. Her father was or had been Albert. Tim knew him – he'd sometimes come into the store on Friday afternoons. A good type. The industrious cow-cocky who rises at four for milking and ends his days in terrible muteness. His children with him milking through every dawn of his life. You could tell it from Lucy Rochester's hands as they held the bread. They

were creased from the milking, the butter churn, and from crank-
ing the chaff-cutter. And then, no doubt, her feet hardened by
walking into school from Glenrock. Falling asleep in the mathe-
matics class. Smartalec children from town laughing at that. He
knew what she didn't. The history of her hard little hands. In the
Old Testament-style flood of '92, the maize crops had been wiped
out when the water swept over the lowlands and lapped against
that embankment where Mr Albert Rochester had this morning
suffered his accident.

From *A River Town*

I've come to the conclusion that, in many ways, ancestor worship, in the broad sense, is one of the universal religions of humanity, and every genealogist, everyone who tells a story about his grandfather, is an ancestor worshipper. The other thing that fascinates me is the story of people on the edge of society, threatened in some way, whether they be Aboriginals as in the case of *The Chant of Jimmie Blacksmith*, Irish immigrants like Tim Shea in that book *A River Town,* or worse still his friend, Bandy Habash, who is from the Punjab.

I'm really writing about the borders between races and the borders between cultures where prejudice always sadly exists, where conditioned thinking about the other group always exists. There's love across this boundary. That's one of the great stories of humankind and I suppose my most noto-rious book, *Schindler,* is about fraternal love across the boundaries of conditioned race hysteria.

———

When I was a kid we were taught the theme of the novel; we had to write this big heading in our exercise books, THEME. And we always thought the writer knew what the theme was. In fact, the writer only barely knew what the story was. He woke up to the theme later. And so I woke up to the theme later also, because it's the story which possesses the novelist. The novelist never says, 'I'll write a book on the theme of two people who fall in love, and they belong to two separate camps.' It's the story of Romeo and Juliet, isn't it? But it's been written again and again and again, not only by Shakespeare.

In fact, novelists always start with the story and of course sometimes it's their own story. But even when it's their own story, fascinatingly, their writing of it alters everything in most cases, even if they say it's a memoir. The writer who told the greatest truth about memoirs was Clive James, when he called his memoirs of childhood *Unreliable Memoirs*.

––––––––

I didn't want to write about the personal, for a variety of reasons. I came from a generation of Australian males who confessed nothing. We were all perfectly happy, perfectly successful; we liked our mates; we were whimsical about wives, mothers and sisters, and we were all utterly sexually fulfilled. And we confessed no insecurity to each other. So I found it hard to write from a personal point of view – but you *always* write from a personal point of view.

You write a book about Australia in 1900, like *The Chant of Jimmie Blacksmith*, and you as infallibly give away everything about yourself as you would have done if you'd written the tale of your marriage.

Gradually, over time, I got more in connection with my feelings. I grew up in a world in which men were not supposed to have a spiritual or an emotional life, unless it was the highly institutional spiritual life and artificial spiritual life of formal religion, and so my journey has been a long journey. Whether it's produced good books I don't know, but it's certainly produced someone who can reveal himself somewhat more than when he started, and although I don't believe in an Oprah Winfrey sort of self-revelation, I think you've got to at least reveal yourself utterly to yourself if you want to be a writer.

Esther Larkin, sitting at some neighbour's fire and hearing the articles of Mitchell read aloud by a hedge-school teacher or pupil, may have looked at her sons and felt a pulse of fear and excitement. But a curse she knew nothing of already lay over these cabins and the companionable potato patches beyond the doors; the fury of God was already moving on the late summer breeze.

The first account of the onset of a potato blight had come to the government at Westminster from the fields of England. There had been a slight earlier rumour from Belgium of a blight which turned the potato flower and stalk black and which caused the tuber itself to putrefy. Sire Robert Pell did not at first believe the report from across the Irish Sea. 'There is such a tendency to exaggeration and inaccuracy in Irish reports that delay in acting on them is always desirable,' he wrote on 13 October 1845.

From *The Great Shame*

A lot of young writers are well advised to write what they know, and to be patient about their experience. That is, their experience will accumulate, and if they don't have anything to write about when they're nineteen, they will by the time they're twenty-three, as long as they don't do something stupid like having a nervous breakdown when their boyfriend or girlfriend leaves, or whatever.

———

Certainly listening to people, picking up on rhythms, is good, but I find reading people is good too. If you want to come up with plausible dialogue, read people's letters, ordinary people's letters. If you're writing, say, about a World War I digger, try to find someone who has the letters of a World War I digger and you'll get the rhythms. I don't think there's a necessity to say, 'This is the day I have to listen to dialogue, so I'm going to spend all morning on the bus and all afternoon in the pub, and I'm going to make notes.' I think you simply pick it up because we are part of this discourse. The writer is not separate from the discourse that's going on in the community, he's part of it.

What young writers have to be careful about with dialogue is to ensure that they're not *all* the one voice. Indeed, writers of sixty-four years like myself have to ensure that all the characters have their own voice. I'm writing a book now; part of it is based on nineteenth-century documents from a female factory in Parramatta and on pastoral documents, and I've been fairly careful to model the style of the letters and journals involved on the style of the time, based on the documents I read.

And then I've got two sisters in the novel who are living in the 1980s and 1990s, so it's one of these annoying books that go on two time levels, and the one sister is scholarly, reserved, a natural puritan, and the other is that well-known creature, the Sydney profane sensualist, and those character differences themselves dictate what they will say. One will say, 'It's hot today,' and the other will say, 'I'm bloody frying today.' That gives you the two dialogues.

———

For most writers, characters won't come until you write. Many of us find out what the book is about by writing it, and many of us encounter the characters by writing them. Of course as soon as we begin to write, we sit there and think, My heaven, what colour hair does this person have? Do they have thick wrists or thin wrists? Thick ankles or thin ankles? And once you start giving them these characteristics, it's almost like the generation of a child in the womb. These few defining aspects of the DNA of the character accumulate exponentially and suddenly there's a physical presence.

———

Those gods and goddesses, everything that's in the Greek myths and the Chinese myths and the Celtic myths, they're all in the cortex of our brains. They are part of our human equipment. And they will emerge by our engaging that part of the mind, but you can only engage that part of the mind by the process of writing. The brain does it for you. The conscious brain says to the unconscious, 'Look, you don't have a respectable job, you've got to sit down in this town or suburb all day and you've got to produce something, so we'd better bring up Athena or Demeter or Apollo or Adonis or Narcissus or Cuchulain or Queen May. We'd better bring them up from the deeps and in an identifiable contemporary, or maybe ancient, form.'

This great sea in which all these ancestors live is also a great computer. There are little blokes who go around saying, 'Athena, you're on. Clytemnestra, it's your turn now.' They pop up like bodies long forgotten, popping up from the bottom of the sea. I feel that in the Australia of my childhood and in the Australia of nearly all Australian men my age, that part of our brain was cemented over. But these wonderful archetypes can penetrate cement, thank Christ.

———

You've got to use the conscious mind to organise material, and sometimes the unconscious is not always the infallible provider of what you should live by. You use your conscious mind in the writing, the shaping, the forming. I always get to a point in a novel where everyone's motivation has just gone to blazes. You've put all these plots up in the air like brightly coloured balls. How to make them land back in your hand? You're baffled, sometimes, by where to take these people and how to resolve all the dogs you've set running. The answers are generally provided, not when you're sitting at your desk trying to work it out, but they'll be provided when you're walking down the street or in a restaurant, or particularly overnight. They'll be provided and there will come a wholly formed solution out of nowhere, because it's come up from the same place as all the drowned gods, sailors, maidens, heroes and ancestors.

———

You can only write a book if you're under the illusion that the world needs this novel, and that no-one has quite written this novel before. You need that degree of obsession to get the thing written. It's no use a marathon runner saying, 'I'll just go for a jog in the park and see how things turn out.' It's no use a novelist doing anything but committing themselves.

One method I use is to dictate. When you can't write any more, go out for a walk with a dictating machine. People will think you're a dog inspector. I live on a beach in Sydney and I've now become notorious for walking along it with my dictating machine. People used to think that I was either mad or spying on them, or reporting them for bringing their dogs onto the beach. If you then transcribe that, you've got something to work on. Something to work on, however flawed, is better than nothing to work on. We're all much better with something down. As primary-school essayists we were better once we got something down, and as novelists we're better once we get something down.

You're going to have to be brave to endure the process, you're going to have to be determined, and you're going to need to maintain this continual connection with your characters. It's better to write two hours a day, four or five days a week. Even if one day you write only fifty words and feel rotten about it, it's better to do that, to be perpetually dwelling with your characters, than it is to take one whole day every two weeks, because by the time you've been away from this process of liberating the archetypes from your head, it's very hard to go back again.

Therefore, be brave. Everyone has gone through the loss of faith in the material. Sometimes the novel dies beneath you like a horse, and when it begins to really smell, bury it. But not until it's really putrid do you bury it.

It is failures of courage which stop the most talented young writers from finishing their books. I can point to many books which are now very well known in the world – for example, Whitney Otto's *How to Make an American Quilt*. Now, Whitney Otto is a brilliant writer, but I can guarantee you that at the University of California, where she wrote that book, she was probably not the most brilliant in the class. The others didn't have the hunger or the temperament to get them through.

The last thing I'd say to the young is you don't have to go to writing school. But if you get the chance to go, go. But you don't have to go and you don't have to come from somewhere posh. Writing has always come from the borders. Look at two examples, Sean O'Casey and the Brontë sisters. Be calm about who you are, but you've got to have courage. That's the only thing.

amit chaudhuri

Amit Chaudhuri, born in Calcutta in 1962, has written two award-winning books, *A Strange and Sublime Address* (1991) and *Afternoon Raag* (1993). Amit arrived in England as a student in 1983. He graduated from University College in London and received his doctorate from Oxford University. His most recent works are *Freedom Song* and *A New World*.

> *When afternoon came to Vidyasagar Road, wet clothes – Piyu's dresses, Bhaskar's pyjamas and kurtas, even a few soggy towels – hung from a clothesline which stretched from one side to another on the veranda of the first floor. The line, which had not been tightly drawn anyway, sagged with the pressure of the heavy wet clothes that dripped, from sleeves and trouser-ends, a curious grey water on to the floor, and, especially in the middle, one noticed the line curved downward, as if a smile were forming.*
>
> From *Freedom Song*

I started writing a long time ago and passed through a long apprentice period as a poet. I turned to prose when I was struggling to find what I really wanted to write about. The struggle is to find where your pleasure lies, as well as what you want to write about. For me they were in two separate compartments for a time. One part of me would write and the other would remember, for instance, with a great deal of pleasure, the visits to my uncle's house in Calcutta when I was growing up. The light, the access to street life, the fact that street life was of importance to me, were in another compartment, but I was beginning to understand that this was my subject matter.

The fact is that there is something in you that delights you in a way that other things don't, and this hasn't been written about because it is you, and you have not existed before.

I'm interested in the off-duty moments – those moments when we're not quite conscious of life – when we're daydreaming, or even at that stage *before* the daydream when we're looking blank and absorbing things. I'm interested in what we absorb as we go through life, and how sometimes those moments have something redemptive about them, but it doesn't come in a flash or in a huge explosion. Those moments are only available in between things and that's what I'm interested in, or have been in my first three novels.

I've never done much research and that's partly because I've been writing about experiences that have belonged to my life. I've had to clear up minor points about Bengali culture or Indian culture or whatever I've happened to be writing about, but I haven't needed to go to the library to do that. I've been able to ask my parents or somebody quite close at hand. Sometimes I've also had to quiz my parents about certain things in their lives.

I used to make notes when I wrote my first novel but I don't these days. They're all there in my head, but I try not to think too much about things because then they seem to lose their surprise.

Memory has a lot to do with a passage like the one I read out – not memory of a certain day or a certain time, but of times that, for some reason I'm not quite conscious of, have impressed themselves on my consciousness. I go back and find out again what it is to live in that moment, and then convey that through those details, not for the sake of trying to give an impression of reality, but because those kind of details exert a force upon you.

So it's to do with that memory, and it's to do with the texture of language. There's a conscious working at leaving out things so that the essentials can remain.

———

With writing there are at least two sorts of difficulties. One is the difficulty of trying to convey what it is you want to convey – in my case a certain physicality and the visual dimension of things – through language. The other difficulty has to do with the conventions and the structure of the novel itself, for which I don't think I'm altogether suited, although I've written four novels. Virginia Woolf said of realist novels that they entail the horrible business of discarding what the character does between breakfast and dinner, or words to that effect, and that's exactly it.

I've begun to feel that I need to look at a form between the novel and the essay and the memoir. Why should I just keep on producing fiction or so-called fiction? That isn't the only way that the imagination expresses itself. There's another problem with me. I'm congenitally an economical writer, in that I say what I want to say in fewer words than maybe I should as a novelist. Being economical is something that I like and admire in other writers, but I think it can be a danger for a novelist, who needs to also sprawl and become boring now and again.

Sometimes the difficult bit is finishing the novel in its first draft. There are things you say in a novel that don't change very much later, but there are the other bits that you work at. Just as a film emerges on the editing table – it's sort of shorn of its bits – so too does the kind of novel that I've been writing. It gives you a great deal of ruthless pleasure to get rid of things that you don't like and let what you do like emerge. That's what it boils down to in the end – your instinct telling you what you like and what you don't like. The nightmare begins when you take out something or add something and the whole structure changes so that you have to do something about it.

Each one of my novels has been something of a nightmare in that sense because there's a lot of cut and paste and a lot of editing behind the scenes, but I find that most of the discoveries I make in the course of writing, and about what I want to say, happen at the stage when I begin to cross out or take out.

———

The thing that has mattered most to me in a story is less to do with the plot – with getting from point A to point B or to Z or whatever – it's more to do with the way I am surprised by the way language is able to convey something about reality; when the novel has passages in it in which you have an altered perception of reality. I don't mean that in a kind of mind-altering, drugged or surreal sense – I mean the transformation by language of something that's quite ordinary into something which is rich. It's the way writing can capture a moment and what inhabits that moment, and transform your perception of it.

> To the people in the house, the clothes formed a screen or curtain which threw shadows and provided bewitching glimpses of the speedy criss-crosses of the grill, and through those criss-crosses bits of the balcony of the house opposite and the sky and the shajana tree, all of which surprised by still being there. The slow leaking of the drops of water from the clothes and their casual, flirtatious flutter with every breeze would not have been noticed by the passer-by on the road, who, if he had looked beyond the remaining leaves on the shajana tree and the iron nerve-pattern of the grill, would have seen them suspended there stilly, like ghosts or patches of colour.

From *Freedom Song*

I didn't consciously create a poetic style, but there is a certain degree of concentration and revision and work needed to convey images. It's not as if you just think about something and then put it down on paper; often you need to take out certain words before the force of another word can come through. So there's an element of consciousness, but not self-consciousness, involved, an element of instinct and working at it.

―――――

When I say that a character in a story is different from one in real life, I don't mean that the real character doesn't have a moustache while the fiction character does, or that the real character is nasty to his children while the fiction character isn't. The fiction character has to exist in a separate sort of mythologised space. The character in that fictional space has a different existence altogether than the real character, though he might be almost the same in terms of habits and features and everything else. It's not a portrait, it's something else.

I came across this distinction when I was reading in a dentist's waiting room an old copy of *Reader's Digest*, which had something by Margaret Atwood in it. She's been both a poet and a novelist. She said that a poet lifts a rock and looks at what's underneath – the insects or whatever – with fascination, and then puts down the rock very softly. The novelist lifts the rock and prods the insects to see what's going to happen next.

For me, lifting the rock has been of even greater interest than prodding the insects, so for me, I suppose, the division between reality and fiction is not that clear. The fictional is always presenting itself to me in real life around many people that I know, so when I'm writing about that, and I seem to be writing about real life, I'm also writing about the quality of fiction I see around me in real life.

―――――

When I started writing my first novel in 1986, the market was not such a big thing in one's consciousness. You had in your mind dead writers and the magic that a work of prose or poetry can achieve, but the market wasn't that much then. It's now quite a big thing, especially for Indian writers. The idea of the market is something that I have to shut out, actually.

When a writer can't seem to get a publisher interested, maybe they should start writing something else. If they have doubts about the novel, then they should put it aside for about six months, or even six weeks, and have a look at it again. If they stop thinking about it for a while and then look at it after some time has passed and see it still works for them, then they should have faith that this is something good and that it will probably be taken up by some publisher in the future. In the meantime start writing something else.

If they find that they've really been able to stop thinking about what they've written, and they've kept it aside for six months and come back and find it needs a lot of work or that it's no good, then they should believe that as well, because I think that is a good test. But of course, if you've been thinking constantly about the novel in the drawer during the six months, then you won't have that distance from it, and you'll come back and most probably be depressed by it all over again.

———

If the writer thinks that what a publisher is saying is going to benefit a work, then obviously they should go ahead with it. I suppose all writers these days have some sort of experience of their manuscript being looked at by somebody else and of things being suggested to them. If they've been to a creative-writing class before they go to a publisher, they'll know that you can often benefit from somebody else suggesting a few changes here and there. But basically you need to have your own judgement about it. If a publisher is asking you to change things that you think are not right – if you believe in what you're doing – then you don't make those changes. But I've seen some people who have gone on to make changes and then the publisher has rejected them anyway, and they've got very upset. So why make changes unless you believe that the changes need to be made?

roger mcdonald

Roger McDonald was born in rural New South Wales in 1941. He is the author of six novels: *1915*, *Slipstream*, *Rough Wallaby*, *Water Man*, *The Slap* and *Mr Darwin's Shooter*, which is about history, evolution and religious faith. His autobiographical *Shearers' Motel* was awarded the National Book Council Banjo Award for nonfiction. He has won a number of other awards, including The *Age* Book of the Year Award, and the New South Wales, Victorian and South Australian premiers' awards. His most recent work is the nonfiction title *The Tree in Changing Light*. Roger McDonald lives in Sydney.

A few days later MacCracken went walking the cliffs on the ocean-side of the Heads and saw, away below him, treading the eyelid of the great Pacific, the strange figure of Mr Covington balanced on a dripping block of stone. He was at his barnacling again. But at what risk!

The sea in that place was a wonder of the world. It rose in a bejewelled surge containing many tons of water, and sank rhythmically, relentlessly, draining enormous square boulders.

All was tide. All was deeps. All was the hidden mystery upon which MacCracken's subject took his toes – protected by canvas shoes – and dared his unfathomable life.

From Mr Darwin's Shooter

I start writing a novel because there's an idea that won't let me go. It's not an intellectual idea, it's usually a bad idea, but it won't let me go. It's like a fishhook that sticks into me and I have to serve that idea.

In this case, I was reading a new biography of Darwin. I read there about Covington; I didn't know about him before. Then I went back and looked at the letters and diaries of Darwin and there's a very famous letter where Darwin writes to his sister in 1834, just after employing Covington. He wrote that he didn't like his servant very much but he was well adapted to all his purposes. I read on, trying to find what it was that Darwin didn't like about Covington, and there was no other evidence of that. That left a blank feel for my imagination. I need that emptiness.

We knew vaguely where Covington was born, knew where he died, what he did in Australia. I had a photograph of him and he had to me the look of a battered survivor. That seemed to satisfy my instinct for this character who had contributed so much, who had been an accomplice in the development of the theory through his specimen collecting. If he'd been a convinced Christian, what would this have done to his beliefs? He was an accomplice in a murder in a way – a murder of religious belief. Handling that conflict was my challenge as a writer in developing the character of Covington.

———

I see the writing process as a problem-solving process. The last thing in my mind is a theme. There's a conflict, there's a story, there's the difficulty of evoking and putting into words that whole story. I chose to alternate the book in slabs of time so that we start early, then we fairly soon jump to late, then we come back to early, then we jump to late again. That was practically the last thing that I did before I handed the book over to the publisher.

———

I was lucky with *Mr Darwin's Shooter* because the Darwin archive is available. The edited letters and diaries are published by Cambridge University. They're very expensive books – about $145 each, but a good investment – and you can have three or four of these on your shelf, heavily footnoted, indexed, and so on. As a resource for this novel they were invaluable, but I was writing to serve a fictional purpose because it is a work of fiction. It has a fictional heart, and fictional truth is the purpose of the novel, so you select so that you are not bombarded by detail, as you might be if you opened library doors and simply went in to research the whole field. You pick and choose; you actually can work in a very narrow vein. I wasn't interested in Darwin himself after about 1838 and then again in about 1860. Everything in between didn't matter, so the research was made much easier for me.

I made a conscious craft decision that I needed a language that somehow evoked an older belief, and a language that evoked nineteenth-century rationalism. For that rational language there were Darwin's writings and Darwin's letters. For the other, inspired by the fact that Covington was born in Bedford, which was the home city of English nonconformity and the birthplace of John Bunyan, I went to *Pilgrim's Progress*. I wove in a kind of a reflection of that spiritual world of anxiety, and beautiful landscape description, in *Pilgrim's Progress*.

> *His earliest memories were not of his mother nurturing him, but of a man with golden curls. His name was Christian. He had rosy cheeks and wore a raspberry-red jacket with gold buttons. The light shone through him by day, while at night his colours went dead as mud. On Sunday mornings he flew soaring over a stile and simultaneously looked back over his shoulder and met Covington's gaze with the bottle-brown of a single eye. He made a beckoning gesture with a crooked finger: 'Follow me.' He was made from coloured glass in a window setting, but the boy didn't know that, in his earliest conjecturing of the world, in which everything past the reach of his arms, whether a tree, a horse, a blackbird, or a river, had an existence equal to his own.*

From *Mr Darwin's Shooter*

I can't imagine considering the market. I do know that, for better or worse, it seems to help a book get around if it has a nonfictional handle. I resent that in a way – that this book does have a nonfictional handle and it has helped it get around. Other books I've written are simply novels largely based on rural characters in Australian life, and that's all they are. They're not about some big, well-known event in the newspaper, or some towering figure of contemporary life, or anything like that.

Shearers' Motel is based on my real experience, but if I'd written it down as the real experience it wouldn't have seemed as real, so I shaped it in the shape of a journey over a year. In fact, the time was longer and I went back to the people I'd worked with and I interviewed them about situations I'd experienced where I didn't know the other side of it, so that I developed a more rounded picture.

And then, at the more immediate level, I changed names and I coalesced places, and so on, in order to make this book a much more living reflection of what real life actually is. So fiction and nonfiction are very blurred for me. I can't make a clear distinction between the two. And curiously enough, some of its readers were confused by that too. It was actually shortlisted for the Miles Franklin fiction award and when this was brought to my attention I had to withdraw it from the award, which was good because it got me some publicity that I wouldn't have had otherwise.

———

I felt very self-conscious of the letter 'I' all the time. It just seemed too egotistical. I was brought up as the son of a Presbyterian minister. You don't matter – it's other people who matter more than you – so that's why I avoided that. And I found that I could better weave in the fictional parts. I was more objective in the third person.

———

You must write out of what you know, but you must imagine ahead of what you know. You don't discover this for years and years as a writer, but you're actually creating, ahead of your own experiences, shapes for your life that comes later. That sounds slightly mystical but I don't think it is, because I think we do imagine our lives as we live them. We decide where it is we are going to go next, and that's imaginative.

———

I don't like the term writer's block and I don't believe in it. I don't think you can be blocked. There's something beyond just sitting facing a blank wall – there's something that you haven't got deep enough into in yourself. To reach it you've got to be patient. If that's writer's block, then yes, of course I've experienced it.

———

To me style is like themes – it's something that's not really the concern of the writer. I think it comes out of the voice that the writer uses, which is usually part of the speaking voice. Style is a product of necessity, not the other way around. Style comes out of what you need to say and the rhythm of what you are saying. I'm only conscious of style in a craft sense. Do I adopt a certain way of speaking for some characters and a certain way of speaking about other characters? That's all. I don't worry about style.

I do like to find the right word. I'm always using my thesaurus. In fact, I can often only understand my own feelings, even outside of writing, if I look up the word in *Roget's Thesaurus*. It's such a wonderful book. It makes things clear.

I revise endlessly and I think the editing process is an important part of revision. When I'm talking to people working on pieces of writing I say, 'Give it to somebody else to read, it doesn't matter whether they're a literary person or not.' Often it's better to choose someone who can just give you the honest blunt reaction, but get some advice. Don't just depend on your own bullheadedness.

———

You've got to fail at everything else because then you've only got one option – that's writing. Being hopeless at everything else really is the best qualification for being a writer. That sounds a bit facile, but I mean there's nothing else I've wanted to keep on doing. I like doing practical things – planting trees and all that kind of thing. Being on the land is what I like most away from writing, but that somehow feeds back into my writing life as well.

The advice my mother gave me was to get a proper job, so I'll give the opposite advice. If this is your vocation, stick with it. You'll have some discouragements but you've got to stay with it a long time. So just keep doing it, and if you only find one or two readers of a manuscript and you can't get it published, you've had those readers anyway, you've had that experience. And except for the ego-boosting and the financial reward, which are not inconsiderable, that's the greatest satisfaction that a writer can have, and that is to be read.

janet evanovich

Janet Evanovich is from New Jersey, the setting for her best-selling crime novels. She wrote twelve romance novels before moving into the crime genre. Her crime fiction debut, *One for the Money,* received the Dylis Award, the Crime Writers' Association John Creasey Memorial Award, and was nominated for the Edgar Allan Poe Award. Other titles in her Stephanie Plum series include *Two for the Dough, Three to Get Deadly, Four to Score, High Five, Hot Six* and *Seven Up.* She lives in New Hampshire.

When I was a little girl I used to dress Barbie up without underpants. On the outside, she'd look like the perfect lady. Tasteful plastic heels, tailored suit. But underneath, she was naked. I'm a bail enforcement agent now – also known as a fugitive apprehension agent, also known as a bounty hunter. I bring 'em back dead or alive. At least I try. And being a bail enforcement agent is sort of like being bare-bottom Barbie. It's about having a secret. And it's about wearing a lot of bravado on the outside when you're really operating without underpants. Okay, maybe it's not like that for all enforcement agents, but I frequently feel like my privates are al fresco. Figuratively speaking, of course.

From *High Five*

I'm a very commercial writer. I like to start out with something that's very entertaining, that hooks the reader, that makes them want to turn to the next page, and I also like to start out with something that explains a little bit about my protagonist. I write a series, and there are a lot of good things about writing a series because you have a lot of continuity. The bad part is that every time you open a new book you have to think that maybe no-one has ever read anything in your series before. So I'm always struggling to find that new, unique, exciting, fun way to tell the reader exactly who my protagonist is.

———

I started off as a painter. I was always the kid who could draw and I graduated from college as a painter. Then I got married and I had a couple of kids. I was a stay-at-home mum and when I was at home I realised that I just like to make things. And it was a very liberating experience because it meant that I didn't just have to be a painter – I could try to figure out what it was that I really wanted to do. I tried a lot of things. I tried writing children's books and I was really bad at that. I tried journalism and I was really terrible at that, and eventually I thought to myself, What I really want to do is write a novel, because as I got older I realised that I loved communicating. I like the idea of a very large audience and I found that

I could make people laugh. I had a good sense of humour and I enjoyed that.

I started out trying to write a book and I had no skills. I wrote three books that never saw the New York publishing scene. They're stuffed away in the bottom drawer of my bureau. I collected rejections from everyone, and eventually, after about ten years of this, I decided that if I didn't get smarter about it, I wasn't going to get published. I was going to have to go out and put on pantyhose, which makes me really cranky, and get a job. Someone said to me, 'I understand they're buying a lot of romance novels, why don't you try writing romance?' So I went out and I must have bought about a hundred romance novels, and I read them. I found out that I liked a lot of the romance novels, so I decided I was going to write two books. I was going to give myself this last shot and I wrote one book – sent it off, and got rejected. I was in the middle of writing the second book when the rejection came back, but I kept up and I sent it off and I sold the second book. So then I was a romance writer. I did twelve romance novels in five years.

I wasn't real great at writing all the romantic scenes. I thought they were kind of boring. I liked the chase but I didn't actually like the details of sexual description – it just wasn't my thing. I wanted more action in the book. I felt like my career was a little flat-lined and I wanted to move into a larger format, and because I wrote with so much humour my editors just couldn't see me doing that and I couldn't get a contract. So in the end I had to reinvent myself. I just had to take a step back – took a year off, tried to figure out what exactly I wanted to do, and learned some new skills. I had to do some retooling to move from romance into mystery and came up with the Stephanie Plum, bounty hunter idea.

There are a couple of things that I had to do. One has to do just with the physical art of writing, because when you write a romance novel the romantic relationship is the plot line. And of course when you write a crime novel you have a much more structured plot and you really need to know where you're going. So I had to change my idea of pacing, I had to change my idea of hero/heroine just a little bit. I had to learn all of these things. I did it by analysis. I did a lot of mystery reading. I tried to find out who it was that I liked, what I thought would work for me, what I thought were effective tools that these people had and how they paced their books, because I knew I wanted to do a real page-turner. I wanted to have a very large audience – I wanted to be able to appeal to men, women, young people and old people. It was a very analytic process, this physical business of learning how to write the crime novel.

And then, because I didn't know a lot about crime, I had to go out and find out what bounty hunters did. One of the reasons why I chose a bounty hunter was because a bounty hunter doesn't have to have a lot of formal training. I didn't know anything about law enforcement. I didn't know anything about guns or tracking people down, but it seemed like this was a job that you could kind of get as you went along. You needed a lot of chutzpah, you needed to be good at lying, you needed to be a bit of an actor, and I thought I could pull this off, so this is kind of where I started out.

A lot of the Stephanie Plum character is really me. She's younger and she's prettier and she's slimmer and she's braver than I am, but she reacts the same way I do. We have a lot of the same history. She lives in a place called the Berg in Trenton, New Jersey. Trenton is the state capital of Jersey and Jersey is kind of a suburb-state of New York, so it's a very urban environment. Jersey girls have this persona – everybody knows what a Jersey girl is. She's kind of this gum-chewing, tough-talking, wisecracking woman who has a great manicure and spends a lot of time on her hair, a lot of eyeliner. I understand who she is. When she's confronted with the situation, I sit back and I think, What would I do?

She's not exactly in my generation – she's younger, she's thirty – but I have a daughter who's twenty-seven and so a lot of Stephanie is also my daughter. I think when you're writing it's very important to be true to the generation you're writing in, and so you have to somehow absorb yourself into that particular culture, wherever your character is living mentally. My daughter makes sure that Stephanie is wearing the right shoes and listening to the right music.

———

I think dialogue is really important and when I first started writing, it was something that I didn't do at all. I didn't know how to punctuate and I certainly couldn't write dialogue. So I started acting and this really is how I learned to write dialogue, because actors do exactly the same thing that writers do. You want to show the audience exactly who your character is inside and you do this by gestures. You do it by the way you dress your character, by the way this character walks, by voice inflection, by the way they pause – this is what an actor brings to the audience and this is what a writer brings to the audience. So I learned how to do this and it just translated right over into my writing. I think dialogue is one of my strong suits now.

"You in the pool?"

"Nope. Morelli nailed you when you where in high school. I don't think you'd let a second boinking go to your head."

"How do you know about high school?"

"Everybody knows about high school."

"Jesus." I swallowed the last piece of my last donut and washed it down with coffee.

Eddie sighed as he watched all hope for a part of the donut disappear into my mouth. "Your cousin, the queen of nags, has me on a diet," he said. "For breakfast I got decaf coffee, half a cup of cardboard cereal in skim milk, and a half grapefruit."

"I take it that's not cop food."

"Suppose I got shot," Eddie said, "and all I had in me was decaf and half a grapefruit. You think that'd get me to the trauma unit?"

"Not like real coffee and donuts."

"Damn straight."

"That overhang on your gun belt is probably good for stopping bullets, too."

Eddie drained his coffee cup, snapped the lid back on, and dumped it into the empty bag. "You wouldn't've said that if you weren't still pissed at the boinking stuff."

I agreed. "It was cruel."

From *One for the Money*

I consider the market at every moment. I'm a very commercial writer. My focus is entertaining. I consider myself to be an entertainer and so this is always paramount in my mind. When I created the series, I sat down and I said I wanted a very large audience. I said, 'Where's the hole in the marketplace?' I think that people are very jaded today and we're always looking for that thing that's new. And what I realised was that I could bring what I did well as a romance writer – and that was the chase, the sexual tension, the very broad humour that I had been working with – and I could put it into the crime format. I would find something that was not incredibly new but a little new, something that I thought could be entertaining, and that's what I did with this series.

When I sit down to write I'm always conscious of the reader. The easier a book is to read, the harder it is to write. I labour over transitions – I want that read to be seamless. I don't want to make the reader work. There are many writers who work at just the opposite direction. They're writers who want the reader to think, to slow the reader down so that they can contemplate small things or large ideas.

I have my own agenda running under there, too. I think that, in terms of my books, if the reader sees my agenda, if the reader sees my craft, then I feel like I've failed. I just want the reader to sit there and to enjoy the book and to want to get to the next page and to laugh out loud once in a while. Underneath it all I kind of push my own ideas. This is a story about a woman who has an extended family, who lives in a community that really cares about each other, that has very close ties. It's a very open community of people, a very nosy kind of environment. I kind of poke fun at this little community where everybody is nosy, but I do put it out for the reader to see because I do think there's some value to this. I think there's value to the big family, to this extended family.

————

I do a lot of self-editing. When I sit down to write in the morning I tend to look over what I wrote the day before and to do some editing there. I find that when I'm at about page seventy to a hundred of a new book I have a pretty good idea of who the characters are, who the new characters are and where the book is going. Lots of times I'll go back to page one and rewrite the beginning of the book, because now I know a little bit more about what's going to happen. Even though I work from a very brief outline, I use a storyboard like they do in movies. I still find that frequently I go back and I rewrite, and then when I'm done with the book I'll take maybe a week to go back and to go over it and fine-tune it, and then I start sending it out to people.

The first time I sent a book out and I got all these rejections back, I said to myself, Well, they didn't even read it. The fact of the matter is that you did something wrong. You need to find out what it is. Either the way that you packaged it up and presented it to the publisher was wrong, or you chose the wrong publisher or the wrong agent. Your writing was tedious, your writing was unprofessional, your manuscript was sloppy; it didn't look like a professional had prepared it. You didn't know the market, you geared the book up to the wrong demographic, you didn't write an interesting book, your pacing was tedious. You know you did something wrong with that book. You need to go back and you need to throw that book away. You need to find out what it is that you need to learn how to do better.

If you want to write, if you want to get published, you'll stick with it. It took me ten years to get published, so I just kept going back and looking at books that I loved and trying to figure out why those books were good and my book wasn't.

———

I have a formula like they do in the movies. I really write my books in three acts with a couple of plot points. I use those plot points as places where I can spin the action around a little bit and put something that's a little bit more important in there for the reader – kind of wake them up.

I know where my story is going to go. I know the beginning, I know the end, and I know a couple of points in the middle. What I do is I have a big whiteboard and I plot out chapter by chapter. I write maybe two or three sentences about action that I think is probably going to take place in that chapter, and then that's what I use to start writing.

I find the transitions to be very difficult. Once I'm in a scene, I'm fine. Once I'm writing about action, once I'm doing dialogue, I'm okay, I can run with that. But I spend a lot of time sitting and finding out how to get from one place to the next. I think it's critical because this is what really holds it together – this is what makes it easy for the reader to move on and this is really where I spend all of my time. This is when I need to get the chocolate bars out – when I have no idea how to get from one place to the next.

———

I think I write all of my books with films in mind because, starting out as a painter, I'm a very visual person, and I really see these books as movies. I see them in front of me, I see these people moving from one thing to the next. In fact, I had a very good movie sale. Tri Star bought the first book and is writing a script on it. And I have to say, I really wanted to see it on the big screen. I actually blew up a car in the first book because I thought it would suck the producer in and would look good in a movie.

———

I would say that this is the best thing in the world to do. I mean, you just can't beat it. It's wonderful – you can work in your pyjamas and you can do wonderful things for people and for yourself. You just have to be persistent and you have to be very open-minded and very honest with yourself, and you have to get used to rejection, to taking criticism and to being very analytic. I think that if you can do all those things, you can succeed.

eva sallis

Eva Sallis was born in Bendigo, Victoria in 1964. Her first novel, *Hiam*, won The *Australian*/Vogel Literary Award for 1997, the Nita May Dobbie Literary Award in 1999, and was shortlisted for the *Courier-Mail* Book of the Year in 1999 and the National Fiction Award in 2000. Her second novel, *The City of Sealions,* explores ideas of cultural and communal alienation and belonging. She is a lecturer in literature and creative writing at the University of Adelaide.

As she headed beyond the confines of the known outer suburbs and beyond Mallala, the home of the furthest visited relative, she was evicted from her familiar Australia into a vast, monochromatic land, stitched up with patchy fences, overlaid with weedy paddocks, stubbly paddocks, golds, browns, and more subtle browns. The broken stalks of some rusty-coloured plant stuck up untidily from the bare allotments. Some of them were filled with rusty rolls of wire and dilapidated machinery. None of it was empty enough to be desolate but it was all the worse for that. The joyless and scrambled buildings and the wilting horses on grassless paddocks made it seem emptier than desolation. It was new and it was ugly. Even the dull leaves of the exhausted trees seemed brown. The car roared, the wheels grinding into the road with an inexhaustible energy, the engine shaking her through the thighs and buttocks, soothing, mind-numbing, leading and accompanying her into the unknown.

From *Hiam*

Ideas come from everywhere. When I've got a project actively on the boil I'll be very receptive to anything that can feed into it – dialogue I hear on the train, a comment a passer-by makes, the way a passer-by holds their shoulders, or just little observable aspects of everyday life, the way the light's striking the trees this morning.

Something like that will filter into a scene that may be partly complete, or even just inchoate or embryonic, or a scene that is complete. I'll suddenly think, That will give it a piece of colour or a nuance or a subtle layer that I need it to have. So they come from everywhere and they come in the middle of the night and they come as a synthesis of things that need to happen. What happens when you're working on a project is that it builds up a kind of critical pressure that is exerted upon you, and unless you feed it, it wilts and dies.

———

It's very hard to imitate someone else's style well. If a given writer has exerted such an influence on you that his or her writing is the model to you of perfect style, the attempt to imitate that teaches you a great deal. It's actually like imitating a karate master's style. Your body may not suit it, but learning the way he or she does a particular technique teaches you a great deal about your own body and about what you can do.

Imitation is a very important stage, I think, but pillaging stories from anywhere – all writers do that. That's quite a mature technique.

———

I think skills are divided into several categories, probably two main ones. One of them is craft skill – having good control of language, of sentence structure, syntax, developing a good understanding of the impact of language on a recipient. That's one package of skills that can be learnt. They can be learnt much the same way as you can learn the piano, with practice and with knowing correct technique.

I think there is a bunch of other skills that are enormously useful for writers. They include close observation and a kind of willingness to go where your project takes you, rather than feeling like you've got to control the project all along – a kind of surrender to the project. I don't think that can be taught. I think some writers acquire it and some writers don't.

———

You need perseverance, a willingness to select criticism that's useful and constructive, but a cast-iron disposition towards unconstructive criticism. That's pretty tricky, that's a juggling act.

I actually took myself seriously as a writer once I started getting published. For the first time I thought, This is a legitimate thing for me to be letting myself do, rather than a recreational thing, and that's an important step. I think once a writer has some encouragement to see him or herself as communicating effectively with the readership, it becomes essential to take yourself seriously and to say that time writing is legitimate time, not stolen time. It's not recreational time, it's work time. And that transition is very hard for writers because they usually have day jobs, but to develop as a writer it's essential to take it very seriously.

———

I don't love the first-person point of view, which is odd because it's so popular at the moment. It has the opposite effect on me from the effect that it's supposed to have. The first person is supposed to invite immediacy with the reader and encourage empathy. I find it does the opposite, because for me it has a very restrictive scope within which to work. I always feel much more like I'm eavesdropping or even hearing stuff I shouldn't hear if it's in the first person.

———

I think collecting rejection letters is a very good idea because all writers get them. I remember before I ever got published that I collected them quite proudly. I started sending my work out to publishers at a time when, although I longed for publication, I didn't expect it. I needed that sense of participating in the story of writers, that what you do is suffer the slings and arrows of outrageous fortune. You have your stuff out there and you put up with all this rejection and that's part of what it is to be a writer. So every rejection letter I got, I thought, I'm being a writer.

———

If I have an idea I want to write about, it will often be something quite amorphous or abstract – a clash of cultures, or grief, or something like that. In the case of *Hiam*, I really wanted to write about grief and I also wanted to write about racism.

From there it evolves. It really takes off once a character or characters come to life for me. Once I could really like Hiam as a person, regardless of how much suffering I put her through, I really liked being in her company, I liked seeing where she'd go next. Then it develops its own dynamic. I have to follow where it goes and do what it needs in order for it to fulfil itself as a project. There's no predicting where it's going to go.

Harddiggers with teeth, or beer-bottle tops, can scrape through rock. When Hiam went out that morning to hang the washing she had found herself looking down a roundish hole, three feet wide and three feet deep, carved through meticulously chewed rock. She felt slightly scared of her daughter. What monster could create such marks? She couldn't stop laughing.

Later that night she and Masoud are standing around the hole, shining the torch over its finely scored sides, laughing at their daughter's great work. It is a labour of love for her father. He catches his breath, staring into Hiam's eyes with a twisted smile and pale lips.

'Hiam, I have never even seen Palestine.'

She laughs. 'Better dig then,' she says softly, gently. She glances at him cautiously.

From *Hiam*

When a manuscript is near finished, feedback from the outside is very useful, particularly if it's good, competent, critical and honest feedback. You end up so close to your own manuscript, you don't really know how it reads from a reader's point of view. I can't read *Hiam* and know what it's like from a reader's point of view because I know what I was meaning it to be like – it's a very different thing. So in a sense we're precluded from being readers of our own work, and we do have to trial them on people. It can be a very distressing thing but it is a very important thing to do.

———

I really love it when you know something's worked, when you get inspired by something. You write it down and you just know that this is the gold. This is the real stuff; you didn't plan this, you didn't expect it, but something is there on the page. It's like tuning in with some greater harmony or greater beauty that you don't even know you have the capacity for. It's a huge rush.

Writer's block is usually a failing of confidence. Write every day, even if you concede that what you're writing may not go into your published project. That really does crack writer's block. I have this theory that everyone has a layer of crap that they have to write through before they get to the good stuff, and the longer you stop writing, the more it just builds up, like a sediment. As soon as you start, you've got to write through this rubbish before you get to the good stuff again. So if you're writing every day you'll stay in the good stuff, whatever that happens to be for you.

―――――

Hiam in Arabic means burning thirst and passionate love. It has two meanings and both of those are very appropriate to the character. I also love Arabic names for women that end in a consonant. I think they are very strong kinds of names, and so getting just the right name is like a game. It's one of the fun sides of the hard work because you just play with this name or that name. It's sometimes not right and you try again with something else until you get just the right one, and it's great fun.

―――――

Just write, just let it rip, no matter what it is, no matter where. The only way you'll ever find your voice is by exceeding it or writing stuff that's not in it, and so just let yourself write anything and everything. Most writers will serve a fifteen-year or more apprenticeship, and young writers need to be realistic about that as well as enjoy it.

richard ford

Richard Ford was born in Jackson, Mississippi in 1944. His first novel, *A Piece of My Heart*, was published in 1976. His other works include *Wildlife*, *The Sportswriter*, *The Ultimate Good Luck* and *Independence Day*, which was the first novel ever to win both the Pulitzer Prize and the Pen/Faulkner Award. Richard Ford lives in New Orleans.

> *Ann, in amongst the hydrangeas, and for the first time today looks purely beautiful – pretty enough for me to exhale, my mind to open outward, and for me to gaze at her in a way I once gazed at her all the time, every single day of our old life together in Haddam. Now would be the perfect moment for a future-refashioning kiss, or for her to tell me she's dying of leukemia, or me to tell her I am. But that doesn't happen. She is smiling her stalwart's smile now, one that's long since disappointed and can face most anything if need be – lies, lies and more lies.*

From *Independence Day*

I didn't know I was dyslexic when I was a little boy. I don't know if in Mississippi in the 1950s people knew what dyslexia was. I just knew that I read really slowly. I probably didn't completely realise that I had some sort of dyslexia until I was in my forties, but I did know that when I was reading literature in college – difficult books like *Absalom! Absalom!* by Faulkner and *The Waves* by Virginia Woolf – I really had to slow way down to read the sentences, and Faulkner's sentences were terribly long.

It didn't seem to me to be disabling to have to read those sentences slowly. It was almost as if they were made to be read that way, and it occurred to me as I began to try to be a writer in subsequent years that that was okay, because I read sentences about the speed I wrote them. Not only could I be in command of them, going along at that pace, but my ear and my eye were attuned to all kinds of qualities and sentences that most people who blaze along and read at 1000 words a minute almost never get attuned to.

An American poet named Richard Hugo said that when language becomes merely a mode of communication, it's dying. For me, language was almost *last* a mode of communication. It was a thing I heard, it was a set of rhythms, it was how a word looked on the page, it was long 'a' sounds and fricatives and vowels and consonants. It was something cognitive or denotative. So I thought it was fine for a writer to be attuned to all of those kinds of qualities, and words and language was a plus.

———

I had written a bunch of stories and tried like hell to get them published and hadn't succeeded. So I thought, Maybe publishing isn't going to be in my future. But I still wanted writing to be in my future, at least until I completely failed at it.

So I set about writing a novel that I knew would take me a long time and would not be impinged upon by worries of continual sending out and getting back manuscripts. When it was finished, after five years, I thought, Well I've given it my best – I haven't been afflicted by worries of publishing. If it's any good I'll send it out and it will either get published or it won't. And I sent it out and it got published.

At the same time, it's in my nature to do the task that I set for myself, and from that comes the satisfaction, not the pie-in-the-sky hope that down the line the world would redeem me and publish me. That was out of my control. What was in my control was writing a book. If it got published, and I hoped it did, then that was fine.

———

Gordon Lish, one of the great American men of fiction publishing in the sixties and seventies – a very mercurial guy, to say the least – said to me, 'Look, Ford, you better publish your next book with me or bad things are going to happen to you.' I thought, That's great.

When I got about 150 pages of what would become the beginning of *The Sportswriter* written, I took it to Gordon. I gave it to him on a Friday and I said, 'You don't have to like this but you said to me you better bring this book to me because I'm going to be your publisher.'

My agent called me up on Monday and she said,

'Gordon's turned the book down,' and I said, 'I can't believe he's really even had time to read it over the weekend.'

A burr got under my saddle about this. I brooded about it and when I brood about things I usually take the trouble right to the source. So I said, 'Come on, let's have a chat, you and me.' And he said, 'Ford, I don't have time to talk to you right now.' I said, 'You have time to talk to me. You turned the book down. I'm not trying to get you to take it back again. Did you read it?'

He said, 'Well, I read into it.' I said, 'Oh fine. So I gave you 150 pages. You read how many? Thirty or forty?' He said, 'Thirty or forty.' I said, 'So that's enough to turn this book down?' He said, 'Look, can I tell you something, really heart to heart? Take this book and put it in a drawer and never take it out. This is not a book you can write. You've started on a book that is really not in your power to write.'

That was not news I wanted to hear. I'd written two books that hadn't gone terribly well, and I'd already been told by my agent that this book had better do well or I was sunk. So I didn't think I could put the book away. I thought, Well, I've written this much of it and I kind of like what I wrote.

I went back out to Montana where my wife and I were living at the time and I did put the book in the drawer. I was so vexed and traumatised by what he said to me that I didn't want to work on it for a long time. I thought if I let it sit for six months I could go back to it and face it by June – this was around Christmas time. And that's exactly what happened. I wrote some stories in the intervening period, then I went back to it in June and wrote it. So it's kind of a good story in a way, of overcoming a certain kind of editorial adversity.

————

Ever since I wanted to be a writer I've had the will to make a story. I'm a noticer and a prolific taker of notes. If I see something, I try to write it down because I know I'll forget it otherwise. So when I start a story, while I may not have the story itself, I do have a collation of raw materials – details written in words, sentences that I've heard over time and thought were interesting, descriptions of people, memories of my own. That's the raw material for what will become a story.

I don't try to base characters on anybody. Inevitably, because we're in the world with other people, flecks and bits and pieces and memories of people work their way into what become characters. If I really were to try to write a character based loosely on somebody, that would be a lot harder than making somebody up, because then I would continually be having to be faithful to that real human being. Trying to translate or transmute that person onto the page would be a rather unwieldy process, whereas if I'm just writing a character, I can change the colour of his eyes with the flick of an eraser. I can give a person a limp or a glass eye or a divorce or polio – all I have to do is change the noun. In fact that's what, in part, creating characters is. It's not reporting on life. Life to me doesn't need reporting on.

I don't think I would be very good at doing research for books. Sometimes in the writing of a book I come up flat against something that I just don't know the answer to.

Then I have to hire an assistant to go out and actually dig up stuff for me. But if I don't know, just through the living of my life, enough to write a story, then I usually won't write it. I'm certainly taking the raw materials of things that I make into literature from the experience of just simply being alive. As a guy walking around the Earth, I really try to take a lot in, try to pay attention, try to remember. Maybe I would be a better writer if I was more thoroughly committed to research than I am, but I'm not. It would take the fun out of it for me, actually.

> *On the plane we are in the midwest from the first moment we take our seats. The entire tourist cabin of our 727 virtually vibrates with its grave ying-yangy appeal. Hefty stewardesses with smiles that say "Hey, I could love you once we're down and safe" stow away our carry-ons. Vicki folds her weekender strap inside and hands it up. "Gaish, now is that ever neat," says a big blond one named Sue and puts her hands on her hips in horsey admiration. "I wanta show Barb that. We've got the pits with our luggage. Where're you guys headed?" Sue's smile shows a big canine that is vaguely tan-colored, but she is full of welcome and good spirits. Her father was in the Air Force and she has a lot of athletic younger brothers, I would stake my life on it. She's seen plenty.*

> From *The Sportswriter*

Sometimes I'm lying in bed at night and I think of the most brilliant idea but the light's already off, it's already one o'clock. I'm ready for sleep to come and I don't write it down, and next morning it's gone. I remember that I had an idea but I wasn't moved enough to disrupt my near sleep and write it down. That's just not caring. That plays a huge part in everybody's life. We're really principally human beings, and many things that pass through our heads just don't stick because we aren't paying attention, or because they don't come to us in the right words.

I think in sentences and in pictures, and sometimes an idea will come into my head and its sentence or its picture doesn't appeal to me. I let it go because maybe I'm watching football on television, or maybe I'm staring out the window or getting ready to take a shower. And that's okay, you know. Emerson said, talking about his independence, that he carries this giant with him wherever he goes, by which he means his responsibility to take care of himself and to be independent and self-reliant. I sometimes put my giant down. Sometimes I just don't walk around the house thinking to myself, I'm Richard Ford the novelist, today I need to be paying attention. I just think, I'm Richard Ford. So if things stick, it's quite advantageous. Things that don't – I don't know. I'm sure if I were paying attention I would be richer or a better writer than I am now.

———

To finish a book requires me to read it aloud. By reading it aloud I get to authorise every sentence, which I think is what it means to finish a book. My metaphor for it is, I get the whole book in my head and then I can see every sentence and I can see every period and every question mark, and how many rhythms there are in the sentence and how many times this word is repeated through the story – everything. I get it all. Novels are written over a long period of time and you're never concentrating on the whole book at once, although you may be trying to. You're writing the end and you're concentrating on the end, or you're swamped in the middle and you don't really comprehend the whole book, except at the end.

I used to read them to my wife, but she got so busy she didn't have time for me to do it. Now I read them to myself, which is too bad in a way, because when I read them to her I only had to read them once. Now, reading them to myself, I usually have to read them twice, which is very annoying.

———

I have a terrific editor in Britain. He has a penchant for 'ly' adverbs. I have a penchant for putting them in and he has a penchant for taking them out. He's right and I'm wrong, but I put them into sentences almost by reflex because an 'ly' adverb has a nice rhythm. It has at least a two-beat rhythm – verily, verily, I say unto you. It's always nice to have that extra couple of beats in the sentence, but adverbs usually come after the verb at a point when they do the least amount of good. Usually when you need an adverb, it's because of some defect in the verb that you've chosen. What I find is that my editor goes through and resolutely circles all my 'ly' adverbs, then I go through and start pruning them out, trying to rely more on the verb rather than the aftermath of the verb. I've talked about being a writer as being like Chekhov and having high artistic goals – it often comes down to pruning 'ly' adverbs.

———

The choice of how the story's told – in the first person or the third person – is for me always an intuitive decision that I make right at the beginning of the story. Almost the first sentence that I write comes to the page in the mode of narration that at the beginning seems most agreeable to the material that I envision writing about.

It is a technical strategy that becomes later on a kind of moral measure of the material. I know that when I write in the third person – and I try really hard to write in the third person because in a sort of Protestant way it's harder for me to write in the third person than the first – stories often turn out to be more stern. The distance of appraisal that the third person affords turns out almost always to induce a harder appraisal of the material than would be the case if I was writing in the first.

First person is so personal. Its address to the reader is, 'Listen to me, believe me, what I'm telling you is true.' The third person, because of the distance, almost always gives you a little reserve.

———

My advice for younger writers starting out is to try to talk yourself out of it if you possibly can. It's very much like getting married. If you can't talk yourself out of it then you're going to do it. But there's a lot of adversity out there. You'll end up spending a lot of time by yourself – you'll end up falling victim to the ills that being alone makes you victim to. I have all kinds of phantom illnesses.

Still, it's a course of life which I can say at age 56 has

rewarded me in all kinds of wonderful ways, but I don't think it's for everybody, nor should everybody think it's for them. My view is that it's a victimless crime to try to be a writer. That's not meant to discourage anyone – it's just meant to tell the truth. That's different from discouraging.

You just have to be very lucky. The only way that you can try to narrow the discrepancy between luck and unluck is to work really hard at it.

Sometimes writing's very complicated and sometimes it's a grind, just like any job would be a grind, but I never think of it as being hard because I think to do what Chekhov did in the world is worth doing. Writing's difficulties are subordinated to what your aspirations are. That said, it is complicated sometimes and it is demanding and it is boring and grinding. But what isn't? It doesn't seem to me to be unusually so. I never think writers have a bad life. I think we have a wonderful, easy life.

a. scott berg

A. Scott Berg graduated from Princeton University in 1971. He received a Guggenheim Fellowship for *Goldwyn: A Biography*. His most recent biography is *Lindbergh*, which won the 1999 Pulitzer Prize. He won the US National Book Award for *Max Perkins: Editor of Genius*. A. Scott Berg lives in Los Angeles.

Into the foggy night, Lindbergh sought companionship with the stars. Feeling the tailwinds and deciding that he could afford to expend some gasoline on altitude, he climbed to five thousand feet. "As long as I can hold on to them," he thought, seeing the stars blink through the haze, "I'll be safe." Sleep remained his worst enemy.

Entering the fourteenth hour, cruising at ten thousand feet, the Spirit of St. Louis *flew through a range of clouds Himalayan in height. With no hope of rising above them, Lindbergh became aware of how cold it was in the cockpit. He removed a leather mitten and put his arm out the window, only to have it stung by cold needles. He aimed his flashlight toward a strut of the plane, on which he saw ice.*

He was aware of the danger, as it was already affecting his

> plane's aerodynamics. *"As far north as Newfoundland and in the*
> *cold of night," Lindbergh analyzed, "icing conditions probably*
> *extend down to the waves themselves;" and if he descended and ice*
> *clogged his instruments, he would never be able to climb again. He*
> *thought of changing his course and flying south, around the storm;*
> *but he had to consider how much gasoline that would cost.*

From *Lindbergh*

To me biography is the toughest form of writing. It combines
the two elements I'm interested in most in writing. I love the
research and I love the history. I love nailing down every fact,
but just as important as getting the history right is getting the
drama right. I think it behoves the biographer to tell his tale
as compellingly as the novelist does. Basically we are all story-
tellers. Whether we are fiction writers or nonfiction writers or
poets, we are there to tell a story, and that involves having a
highly readable prose that pulls the story along all the time.

———

What drew me to writing about Lindbergh had very little to
do with aviation. It had to do with Lindbergh the man. It had
to do with the fact that to this day, some seventy-five years
after the flight that made him famous, Lindbergh still
remains a compelling figure. I wanted to find out what was
behind that hero. There had to be a man there.

Here was also a figure who became a great victim within
five years of that flight. That victimisation was a result of the
fame that chased him after he landed in Paris. Just a few years
after that he was accused of being a villain, of being a traitor

to his own country, of being pro-Nazi, of being anti-Semitic. I began to think, How could one person engender so much in such a short period of time? And because the story had never really been told, mostly because his family had never spoken publicly about him and because his papers had been kept under lock and key, I wanted to get to the bottom of it. I wanted to find the man behind the riddle.

———

It took me about nine and a half years to write the Lindbergh story. I'd been doing a lot of general reading before I actively got involved in the book, but once I did, it took me about four and a half years to do the research. It took me two solid years just to get through his personal archives, and then another two years to get through archives of other people, interviews and background reading.

After I'd done four, four and a half years of research, it took me almost a year to sort through all my notes and to lay them out in some sort of dramatic fashion. I found that I had mountains of papers and notes on my desk, but they all sort of fell into chapters. So now into my fifth and sixth years, I began to write. It took me one year to get a draft on paper.

When I write my biographies I remember something that Max Perkins, the great book editor, used to tell his authors: 'Just get it down on paper and then we'll see what to do with it.' So I write my first drafts as quickly as I can. I throw in everything and then I see what I've got. That's the clay I begin to mould. It's got some vague shapes to it because it's divided into chapters and acts by then, but then I really begin the process of cutting, rewriting, rewriting and rewriting, and that takes about three or four years. So all that suddenly adds up to some nine, nine and a half years.

Then, just as important, I think, is the promotion of the book. I think it behoves writers to present their books to the public. In America there are some 60 000 new trade titles every year, not even including textbooks or scientific books. How do you make your book stand out from the pack of the 60 000? I usually take my show on the road and talk about my subject and my book.

––––––

The biographer over a decade sustains himself largely through his interest in his subject. It really does become a great battery for you – it becomes your motor. I've had three extremely compelling heroes to write about: Max Perkins, Samuel Goldwyn and Charles Lindbergh. I can honestly say with all three books I didn't have one uninteresting day. There were some days where the work was more drudgery than not, but something new or wonderful happened every day to me, either in the research, the writing or the rewriting, which I absolutely adore doing. That's the most fun, in fact.

On the more practical level, I was lucky that my very first book, about a completely obscure literary figure, Maxwell Perkins, became a bestseller. Publishers then began to realise that maybe Sam Goldwyn, whom we have heard of, would sell even bigger, and Charles Lindbergh, who was a world-famous celebrity, would sell even bigger. So since my second and third books I've received rather good advances. My Lindbergh book received a seven-figure advance. My publishers give me a payment up front, then they pay me a yearly stipend and then there's a balloon payment at the end, so I can live fairly comfortably over ten years.

———

I keep looking for the newfangled way of taking notes for a biography. Every time I see a biographer I say, 'Have you found a way to collect the data and to organise the data on a machine?' And all of them say you can't. It seems to me you have to do it the old-fashioned way. I use five-by-eight, colour-coordinated note cards. I divide each colour on each book according to certain other subjects within the book. I usually then organise the notes chronologically. The reason why I think it's important to do it on cards or on sheets of paper, and why it cannot be done mechanically, is that sometimes when I'm sitting down to write a chapter, or even a paragraph, I will have a hundred different note cards before me on my desk. I shuffle them and reshuffle them and move them around and do this and that, and then I write my paragraph. Sometimes I will draw three bits from the hundred cards and sometimes I will draw one hundred bits from the hundred cards, but I need them all before me. The only way I know how to do that is to have the hard copy there.

———

There are various schools of writing biography. Many biographers are extremely subjective. Some decades back, psychobiography, in which the biographer would put his or her subject on the couch and analyse the subject, became very popular. It was usually not very effective, and usually a little cruel.

I'm of the school that believes biographers should be as objective as humanly possible, and that means approaching the truth. I'm fully aware that truth is multi-faceted. The one thing that I've learned about the truth over my thirty years in writing biography is there is no single truth. What I try to do, though, is let others present the truth. I think of myself, when I'm writing a biography, as a choral conductor. As I'm telling my story, playing the themes of my subject's life, I'll say, 'I need a few violins here, I need to bring in Mrs Lindbergh here, I need to bring in my cello now, I need to talk to Charles Lindbergh's youngest daughter here,' and I pull a voice in and modulate one voice over the other. In that regard, I think by having as many voices as possible, by having this choral response to my subject, a kind of truth emerges.

The other metaphor I often think of as I'm doing my books is that I often feel like the photographer who's developing film in a tank. He dips the paper in and the picture gets more and more real, more and more clear, increasingly vivid. There is a kind of truth there. When I speak of truth, I really mean that the author doesn't let his or her own biases creep in. That to me is the most important thing.

For the next few minutes, as the wind pulled his plane every which way, he followed the clearest path that presented itself, heading south whenever that option existed. At one point he found himself turned completely around, in quest of safe passage. Soon the coating of ice thinned. He observed that both his earth-inductor compass and his liquid compass overhead were malfunctioning. His only hope for getting across the watery abyss lay in the hairline needles of those compasses pointing the way. Lindbergh could only deduce that he was entering a magnetic storm, which he would have to ride out navigating by instinct.

Just then, heavenly assistance arrived. Not only did the expanses between the great thunderheads of the storm widen, but moonlight appeared. Its unexpected illumination disoriented Lindbergh at first, because in shortening the night – racing with the earth's rotation – he had not correctly reckoned when it would show up. Taking off from Roosevelt Field in the early morning had assured Lindbergh the maximum of daylight hours; as it was, he faced but two hours of solid darkness.

From *Lindbergh*

I've written three biographies now and I can honestly say I've not censored myself because of an issue of propriety. I remember in my Goldwyn book I came across an unseemly story about a secondary character which I wrote in my initial draft, and then I cut it. I didn't cut the story because I thought it would be offensive to anybody, or that it might ruin a life. I cut it because it didn't make dramatic sense – it wasn't really about my protagonist, it didn't advance the story. Had that story applied to my protagonist, I would have included it.

My subjects are dead, so I feel that their lives are lived. What they did could or should become part of the record. I've never had to face an instance in which I've encountered a story or a fact that might ruin somebody's life. I would certainly have to think long and hard about that if it would.

I don't think the biographer's job is to be sensational or to hurt. This gets back to telling the truth. I've had a few episodes in each of my books that really surprised the children of my subjects. At first, a few of them were slightly offended, but in the end they were rather relieved to know of them. I'm thinking of a love affair in the case of the Lindberghs, a thwarted love affair in the case of Sam Goldwyn, and a platonic love affair in the case of Maxwell Perkins. In all three instances the children were taken aback, and they all called me in dismay and shock. A week later they all called up and said, 'Thank you so much for putting that in the book. It has really clarified things for us.' I think ultimately the truth does set you free.

———

I love revising for two reasons. First of all I love the sheer mechanics of it. I love figuring out the proportions of a book, and that's the hardest thing a biographer has to do. That's the part where he's chiselling the clay; that's the part where he's really weighing every piece of evidence and saying, 'How much weight does this deserve in this particular story?' It's also a great artistic moment in the book because that's the moment where I get to weigh each word.

To me, the happiest days are those where I can spend an hour just working on a sentence, polishing it, or maybe two or three hours getting a paragraph just right. That's a great artistic turn-on for me. I'm a writer – I love spending my life with words. I love playing with them and seeing the power of them. Sometimes I can see that moving a sentence from the end of one chapter to the opening of a new chapter will completely affect the rhythm of that part of the book. Those are really wonderful decisions – they're almost musical decisions.

I worked on my Lindbergh book with rather a gifted editor. She was reading my kidnapping chapter and she said, 'I think you're missing one or two beats here and here.' And I thought, That's the perfect thing to have said to me. She didn't have to say another word. The music was off, the beat was off, and that was all I had to add. It felt wonderful when I did.

———

I think this is the best of times and the worst of times for biography. There's a lot of tabloid biography going on now – pathography almost. It's really just raking over the dead organs. But at the same time I think there are a lot of new and young writers who are going into the biographical arena. Part of the reason, at least in the States, is it has been lucrative for a lot of people.

I think it began to come into fashion again really in the seventies and eighties. I remember talking about this resurgence of nonfiction, and especially biography, to one of Max Perkins' novelists, a woman called Marsha Davenport, who'd been an extremely successful novelist in the thirties and forties. She said that good fiction comes out of a trusting nation, and that was the case in the thirties and forties. She said that we're no longer a trusting nation. We want to know what's going on. We want to know not only what's going on now, but also what was really going on then. That's the reason for history.

I think biography is the most compelling form of history because you're basically following a drama. You're following a character through history, and for that reason I think the last twenty-five years have been very good. I've seen a great number of good new biographers coming along. I still consider myself coming along, for that matter.

———

The best advice that I can give biographers is to read other biographies and see how it is done well and how it is done badly. There's also a lot to be gained by reading good drama. Getting a good sense of how a well-made play works, of dramatic structure, is extremely valuable.

I also think how much of the background is being revealed is what separates good biographies from bad biographies. I think there's so much to be learned for a biographer by reading the newspapers of the day. On each of my books I spent days, weeks at a time, reading old *New York Times* from the days that things were going on. On the day Charles Lindbergh landed in Paris he filled the entire front page and front section of the *New York Times*. But what about the days before that and the days after that? What were the advertisements like? What did an apartment, a penthouse in Manhattan cost then? What did it cost to buy a chicken for dinner? What was the weather like? What boats were shipping in and out? What were the other news stories that show what the world in which my character walked was like? I think that's the most crucial thing we as biographers can do.

ann-marie macdonald

Ann-Marie MacDonald was born in Germany. She is a writer
and actress and has appeared in many plays, television dramas
and feature films. Her novel *Fall on Your Knees* won the 1997
Commonwealth Writers Prize for Best First Book. Her play
Goodnight Desdemona (Good Morning Juliet) won Canada's
Governor-General's Award and has had more than fifty pro-
ductions worldwide. Other works for the theatre include *The
Arab's Mouth* and the libretto for the internationally acclaimed
chamber opera, *Nigredo Hotel*. She lives in Toronto.

*Here's a picture of Daddy. He's not dead, he's asleep. You see that
armchair he's in? That's the pale green wingback. His hair is
braided. That's not an ethnic custom. They were only ethnic on
Mumma's side. Those are braids that Lily put in his hair while he
was asleep.*

*There are no pictures of Ambrose, there wasn't time for that.
Here's a picture of his crib still warm.*

Other Lily is in limbo. She lived a day, then died before she could be baptized, and went straight to limbo along with all the other unbaptized babies and the good heathens. They don't suffer, they just sort of hang there effortlessly and unaware. Jesus is known to have gone into limbo occasionally and taken a particularly good heathen out of it and up to heaven. So it is possible. Otherwise . . . That's why this picture of Other Lily is a white blank.

From *Fall on Your Knees*

I started out as an actor. I trained at the National Theatre School in Canada and when I came out of that training process I moved to Toronto and I started acting. Within a year I had done all the things that a young actor is supposed to do. Then I started working collectively and collaboratively to create shows, and from working collectively and collaboratively I started writing shows on my own and acting in them. At a certain point I found that I was writing something that I wasn't going to act in, a play called *Goodnight Desdemona (Good Morning Juliet)*, and that was a turning point. I've written a libretto for a chamber opera, I've just finished a script for a musical comedy, and I'm also working on a book.

So what was most important to me? The same thing that was most important to me as an actor, and that is to tell a story. I'll be a channel for the stories that want to get told, the stories that want to be born, and they tend to tell me how they want to get told. When I started working on *Fall On Your Knees* I thought it was a very bad play with really long stage directions and monologues. I thought, No, I don't cop out and write monologues, I write dialogue, I have lots of people on stage, I do the hard thing. I thought, Why am I suddenly writing monologues and stage directions? Then it was revealed to me that it was fiction, and when I realised that, I was suddenly unblocked and I found my way into this world and it took years to unfold. But the stories are kind of like kids – they are who they are, and if you give them the wrong name they'll let you know. Send them to the wrong school and say, 'You're going into the army,' and they say, 'No, I'm going to be an artist.' They tell you what they want to be.

My background as a playwright and an actor is my biggest single influence. I think of my book as a performance when I'm writing it. I try to inhabit the characters. I try to essentially play each and every one of those roles. It's very important to me that each and every character has a journey that is complete. I have to feel as committed as an actor to these roles, regardless of their size and also regardless of whether or not it's comfortable. It was very uncomfortable to inhabit the role of the father in this book, but I had to do that. I have to find the empathy and the compassion and the love to see the world through those eyes, or I'm writing something judgemental rather than something that is emotionally true.

———

At the beginning I saw sepia tones, that kind of yellowed photograph look, and it's a kitchen table. Okay, it must be an old photograph. Pull back a little bit (living in the twentieth century, it's hard not to think in filmic terms), so we pulled the camera back a little bit – oh, it's a house, it's a clapboard, it's white. Pull back a little bit more, it seems to be on this sort of scrabbled, tough landscape. Pull back more, it's an island, and you think, Oh my God, I know that island, I know where that is, and now I know when it is. This house is where I'm going to start, and I'm going to start with these people, and I know there's a garden and I know there's a secret in the garden. So I think I follow very much the reader's journey; I ask questions and I try to make the discoveries, and then once I've figured it out, I go back and I try to write it so that it's approachable by somebody I don't know, and that's the reader.

———

Having written a lot for theatre and also for television in order to support the writing of *Fall on Your Knees*, I knew quite a bit about structure. I knew how to build a story, and in a way I tried to forget that because I thought, If I go on that skill, if I go with that knowledge, I might miss something really organic or surprising. I have to forget that I know how to plan it out, forget that I know how to build something.

I liken it to having focused on creating all the vital organs and the mucous membranes, and then eventually the central nervous system. Finally, once I have this soft creature on the slab, I stick the bones in it. It was hard to put the skeleton in at the end, but it was worth it because I knew that I had the vital thing. I knew I had that beating heart and that was more important to me.

Obviously the structure is of tremendous importance

and that takes a lot of skill and a lot of commitment, and I love that challenge. It's like playing a big chess game in your head. That was something I committed to, but I deliberately did it last.

———

I had early on identified a challenge of trying to make sure that I wasn't in this book, to remove myself from it, by which I mean remove my own attitudes, showing off, anything that reeked of cleverness, or self-consciousness – watch me turn this phrase, or 'I've thought about these deep things and I seem to have summed it up rather well.' Anything like that I removed with the tweezers or with the knife.

The first year's work on this book ended up in the bin. If I'd known that starting off, I might have found it very discouraging. It's not that it was garbage, it turned into something else. It got distilled and boiled down, but mostly what I removed was myself.

———

As an actor you can speak and you can move and you can show, but you can't tell the audience things except by a series of really awkward asides. I try to apply the same rules when it comes to fiction. If somebody is having a searing emotional experience I would say that they pick up the fork instead of the spoon. I would try to externalise it and make it into an action. Make it into something that someone could observe. You don't have to be inside that person's head to know what they're going through. Why would they pick up a fork when they clearly need a spoon to eat that soup? I find that more moving anyway, because it's not like sending a telegram to the audience.

> *Mahmoud was in bed and out like a light at the other end of the room. Frances stood at her late grandmother's vanity and surveyed the loot laid out before her. Silver brushes, combs and hand mirrors. A rosewood jewellery box. She lifted the lid and up struck a hurdy-gurdy orchestra along with a pink ballerina. Frances shut the box instantly and turned back towards Mahmoud, who groaned, rolled over and looked straight at her. They just stayed like that, staring at each other, until she realized he was still asleep. She waved at him. She gave him the finger. She returned to the jewellery box and opened it a hair's breadth – yes, now she could see the little dancer lying flat on its face. Frances slipped a finger through the crack and pinned the thing in dead-swan position while she opened and plundered the box.*

> From *Fall on Your Knees*

My way in was to start with the first person. That was my way into the characters and that was very important, but I soon realised that I wasn't going to be able to exercise the narrative scope that I wanted if I stayed with that. So for me it was a device, it was an entry point, but I didn't stay there.

That said, I don't have an objective voice; the voice shifts sympathies. I often talk in the third person, but from the point of view of the character who is most central in the scene at hand. That third person's voice has to shift to give weight to that point of view. So to me it's not so much about my voice as an author, it really is, Where's my point of view? Where's the camera, where's that pair of eyes that is guiding the reader through this story? The closer it gets to one person, one particular character, the more intimately it's going to reflect that character's attitude.

———

I think that even when you're stalled or suffering from writer's block there's a lot of writing going on – you just can't get it out, and that's where you really have to be patient and have various strategies. You have to sort of sneak up on your mind and ambush it; that means reading, or going for a walk, or doing something that you thought you dreaded, which in fact unlocks something or triggers something. In other words, get into life, loosen up a little bit, and then maybe you can scare up something from the back of your mind.

———

What I always look forward to is when I get to the place where the work and the idea is bigger than me; it's bigger than my ego, than my ability to write it. The whole point of writing is so that I don't own it, so that it ceases to belong to me and it belongs to everybody who reads it. When people talk to me about it, I sometimes have a curious experience of feeling detached, like, 'Why are you asking me what it means? Yes, I created it, but it's not mine any more, it's everybody else's.' I don't obsessively read it and I don't refer back to it. I've given it away.

———

For me, continuing to write for theatre and music is very healthy. It's kind of an artistic crop rotation – it puts things in perspective. It allows me to be less precious and pressured about my next novel, thinking, What are the readers expecting? Will they like this, is it too much like what I did before? You forget it, actually, and if I'm surprised and engaged, then they will be – that's the whole point. I have to return to the place where I'm going to be mystified or amazed or excited or engaged by a story that's unfolding.

———

For young writers it's important to be hungry for experience and for knowledge, and not just the kind of narrow knowledge of what it means to be a writer. What it means to be a writer is simply a result of an attitude to life, which is to pay passionate attention to what's going on around you and not to focus so much on being a writer.

When it comes down to actually writing, have faith and a lot of patience, because things that arrive in a blaze of glory and inspiration take a great deal of time and start to feel very pedestrian. That's when you really have to stick with it, because so much of writing doesn't happen in that first flush, it's a marathon, and it's about faith and patience more than anything else.

john lanchester

John Lanchester was born in Hamburg in 1962. He was brought up in the Far East and educated in England. He has been a columnist and a board member of the *London Review of Books*. His first novel, *The Debt to Pleasure*, won the Whitbread First Novel Award, among others. His most recent novel is *Mr Phillips*. He now writes full-time and lives in London.

One tall boy in the queue has a tiny pink rucksack with yellow straps and fittings with the word 'Sexy' picked out in lime-green sequins. His hair is shaved at the sides and he wears a T-shirt with capped sleeves. He looks very fit, at least as fit as Mr Phillips had been at the end of his school days, when he had been fitter than at any other point in his life. Walking past the queue is a girl from the lower deck of the bus. She is wearing the shortest skirt Mr Phillips has ever seen; so short that the lower part of her buttocks are visible at the top of her thighs. The flesh there is slightly mottled, not quite with nodules of cellulite – she's too young for that – but with a curious pale, corrugated texture like that of chicken skin. She also wears clogs and a pink T-shirt. Her brown hair is cut so short that her top vertebrae have a knobbly prominence. Her appearance gives Mr Phillips a pang of envy that girls in his day had not dressed like that and a near-simultaneous twinge of relief, since if they had he would never have summoned up the courage to talk to them. She does not so much walk off as totter, making one or two smoothing-down gestures at her skirt, about which she seems with some justification to be a little self-conscious. Perhaps she has grown taller since the last time she wore it. Certainly it is well within the category of what Martin would call a 'pussy pelmet'.

From *Mr Phillips*

In a sense any story is a rhythm of withholding and revealing. But withholding something fantastically important that has happened to a character, that the reader discovers in the course of the book, has to be handled with some care. It can be irritating and distracting, and can make the reader feel conned. It's one of those many things where there's a subtle sense of what's cheating and what isn't. I think it's about thirty or forty pages before it is absolutely clear through many signs in *Mr Phillips* that there's something odd going on with him. I hope it's not a rabbit-from-a-hat thing, but a gradual revelation of the secret, which is a slightly different technique. I suppose you really have to use these things with some moderation because otherwise they turn into pure trickery, which, I think, is to be avoided.

————

I did a fair bit of research for *Mr Phillips*. I picked up quite a lot of impressions of London from living there for ten years or so, but I did research things like the route in the book. At one point he goes over Chelsea Bridge and then takes a right. There isn't a bus that does that, and I thought of various things like him walking across and waiting on the other side. Then I thought, Oh, life's too short, and I made the bus up. But apart from that, it's fairly accurate. The book is set in 1995, so quite a lot of those things are already matters of historical fact. Cities change so fast – lots of things about London, as about any city, have already changed in those five years.

———

First person is a dominant mode in contemporary fiction. Because the narrators identify themselves, you trust them more. I think it's part of a general scepticism about authority and a voice from on high which won't identify itself.

I wanted to try to use the third-person voice, not to look down at the character, but to get alongside him and to partly describe his world rather than just catch his voice. Also, my first book is in the first person and I wanted to try something different. The effect that I was looking for was to create a kind of intimacy by abolishing some of the distinctions between 'this is me talking', which is the first person, and 'that's him over there', which is the third person.

———

The talent for writing and the ability to write is far more widely distributed than the ability to finish books. I know a lot of extremely talented writers who won't finish books.

Lots of people have the ability to sit on their bums for

very, very long periods, and there are people who have the ability to write, but they're often not the same ones. I think it's quite hard to cultivate the former – that's partly why I have to concentrate very hard on making myself write every day. Otherwise I tend to wait for lots of inspiration, and it doesn't work like that for novels. You have to work on novels every day. I get big, up-and-down mood swings in the course of writing, but I just have to treat them as if they're weather and ignore them and keep going. For me that's the answer – it's a learned technique. Ignore all those voices in your head and just keep plugging away. I don't find that hard any more because I've learned that you just have to keep doing it every day. I do it on a word-count basis.

———

My favourite bit is plotting out and thinking about what I'm going to do next. You can do anything you like. You're free in your head – you can wander anywhere. Actually getting into the book is like wandering about in the open, then going under an overhang and finding exciting Aboriginal paintings on the wall. You go slightly further in and it's slightly darker, but there's still interesting stuff there. Then you go further in and you realise you're actually in a tunnel and you can't go back. You've got to go on, but now the tunnel is narrow, dark and more cramped, and there's a point at which you're locked into it. You've got to finish but you've suddenly thought of seven other books you'd rather be writing. These other ideas sit there going, 'Write me, write me,' but you have to tune out and go through the tunnel you stumbled into in the first place. So there's a sense of narrowing possibility and having to finish it – of being past the point of no return.

I do a lot of plotting and planning in advance mainly out of laziness – because of not wanting to go up a blind alley and lose a few months' work. I know lots of people think the exact opposite, but I try to structure pretty much everything that happens in the book and then I'm taken by surprise by the texture of it. It's basically a way of tricking yourself. You think about one thing in order not to think about another. I think that writers think about the plot in order to let the language come through the unconscious, or they think about the language all the time and let the unconscious write the plot.

For example, P.G. Wodehouse's notebooks show that he never thought about the language and the jokes in his books – all the notebooks are about plot twists. It's clear that that was his sort of distraction, and he could do the other thing partly because he was distracted. I think that's a sort of allegory for what most people do. With me, conscious thinking is very much with plot and structure in order to let the sentence-by-sentence things well up.

————

I don't think much in terms of reader interest, I think in terms of the internal mechanism of the book. I think of the structure as having things pulling it in slightly different directions, and that keeps it tense in the way that a living thing is always tense. For instance, in my first book the plot momentum was accelerating and the language, because it was quite rich, was slowing down. I was very aware that the plot made you want to read quicker and the language made you want to read slower.

In my second book, *Mr Phillips*, it seems as if a lot happens, but in a sense nothing happens. I was very aware of wanting to have that balance, just as in life, when in a sense nothing happens and in a sense everything happens all the time.

Mr Phillips was a predicament before he was a character. I was thinking about the situation of a man who's lost his work – his identity is all wrapped up in his work and he's suddenly made redundant. I knew the trouble he was in, and he grew from that. He was his situation before he was fleshed out into his personality.

This morning, Mr Phillips has just woken from a seven out of ten dream in which he was trying to arrange to have sex with Miss Pettifer, his younger son Thomas's form teacher at St Francis Xavier's. She is in her early fifties and therefore around the same age as Mr Phillips. In real life, he hasn't been conscious of being even vaguely attracted to her – but when he wakes after the dream, he realizes that isn't the whole story. The fact that she is, say, twenty pounds overweight, he feels in part of himself as a liberation, as if, in throwing off one set of worries about being sensible and watching your weight, other worries might be thrown off too, so that her half-double chin and wildly blossoming hips, all the more visible because her clothes are a third of a size too small, hold a promise: with me, you can do anything you want.

From *Mr Phillips*

I do the revision at the end. I write in longhand and when I get to the end I go back and type it into a word processor. It's actually excruciating – I don't quite know why I do it. I think it's because I don't reread as I go along, I just keep plodding forward and then suddenly see it for what it is. By that point I've been doing it for a couple of years or more and there's all sorts of intense mixed feelings, because while I'm typing it out I'm dreading it being unusable.

I revise as I type it out, then print out the draft and go over it. One of the great things about the word processor is that you can make quite radical changes if you suddenly realise that something belongs somewhere else.

I do one very, very thorough rewrite and then go over it checking for specific details. I find it useful to print it out not in double space, but as it would appear in a paperback, to look at it for pacing. You can get so fixated on sentence-by-sentence and paragraph-by-paragraph points that it's actually hard to remember how the pacing works.

———

I suspect the situation in Australia is the same as it is in Britain and America, and that's that publishers have stopped reading unsolicited manuscripts – what they inelegantly call the slush pile. For example, about three years ago, my publisher Faber published a novel about Genghis Khan and that, they said, was the first book they'd taken off the slush pile since *Lord of the Flies*, which was published in 1954.

There are exceptions – Roddy Doyle is the most famous one in British publishing at the moment. His first, *The*

Commitments, was taken off the slush pile. So it can be done, but in general the best advice is to get an agent. It's very frustrating when people don't get published, but in Britain we publish 100 000 books a year – it's gone up enormously – and that means that everyone's got a chance.

———

I don't think about the market at all. There's no quite so reliable way of losing your bearings, because if you think about the market, you try and second guess it, and the market doesn't know what it wants until someone comes and shows it. People can only think about things that already exist, but the whole point of it is to try and make something new.

neal drinnan

Neal Drinnan was born in Melbourne in 1964. At seventeen he abandoned his education and suburban family home for the lure of life's more ephemeral things. He has worked in publishing for many years and has been a frequent contributor to a number of magazines. He is the author of three novels – *Glove Puppet, Pussy's Bow* and *Quill*.

Des's lot were too busy with their jobs, kids and new house, so they couldn't get to her very often, and Rose hated planes – or at least she knew she would if she ever got on one. Three days on the train to Western Australia she just couldn't come at. You never imagine life will pick people up and take them so far away – Perth, New York. Your own children moving as far away as possible. What have they got in those places that could make a family scatter so? *It just didn't seem fair. She sighed.* 'All God's children have walking shoes,' *she remembered from somewhere in the Bible, or from a lost sermon during her youth. She supposed grief to be another of her lessons but it was an enormous burden and it had worn her down. The Lord seemed to save his biggest tests and*

greatest cruelties until you'd no spirit or strength left to bear them.
Life all seems back-to-front, *she thought quietly.*

From *Quill*

For the type of novel I like to write, I think having a strong sense of the evolution of the story is important. The denouement is a really important thing for me. Before I start writing a novel, I have to know what it is I'm setting out to do. I have to know, in reasonably traditional terms, that there's going to be a climax, or a couple of climaxes to a story. I'm really keen to set up a certain kind of intrigue at the beginning of the book and follow that through so that most of the ends are tied up. I am a little bit formulaic in that I like intrigue and I like suspense.

The ability to develop mystery is a talent that comes from reading a lot, and from having a genre of literature that you like or that you see as having utilised those things successfully. There are always books that completely have me in. I'm always dreaming of writing books like that. I'd love to be keeping people up at night. So I think that you can study a broad range of writers and see how they create that suspense.

———

It's important for me to plan out a basic structure. I'd be a bit nervous about starting something if I didn't have the basic storyline in my head, but once that's done there are many, many thousands of words that go off in tangents. The characters evolve in ways that I hadn't necessarily bargained on before I started, and that's fantastic. There's something organic happening that surprises me even as I'm writing. That's the fun part of writing and the chaos of it. I still usually end my stories with the same structure that I had in mind at the beginning – it's just that the characters have become more complex, as they should the better you get to know them.

————

In my second book, *Pussy's Bow*, there's this roguish Englishman who's terribly charming, terribly witty and terribly clever, but he rips people off. He's a user and even though he does all these things, people still like him. I based him on someone that I met ten years or so ago in England who I became quite good friends with. He stole my credit cards.

There are always things in my own experience that I can employ. I'll think, Yeah, I'll make that character like him. Otherwise I would just use the emotional experiences that I've seen other people have. The characters evolve partly out of observation and partly out of a component of myself. I think there's something of me in all the characters that I write about.

I think it's a truism that it's good to write about what you know, especially if you're given to concentrate a lot on emotional issues. It's hard to write something that you've never actually felt yourself, but obviously there are lots of people who write extraordinary flights of fantasy. So far I haven't gone too far like that in my own writing – I tend to use emotional scenarios that I've witnessed or I have some experience of.

The pictures had sat in Dixon's wardrobe for a week. He'd really just meant to borrow them but he couldn't see the harm in at least letting a gallery appraise them. Dixon vaguely knew Merrily Davis. Her gallery was downstairs in the same building as his office. While she possessed the accoutrements and manners of a charming Toorak matron, Dixon suspected butter wouldn't melt within a mile of her mouth.

This became apparent the minute he indicated he was there to sell something, not buy. The shift in demeanour almost frightened him.

'Merrily, I have been given two Dũng Ngo's, which I'm terribly fond of, but you see I'll be travelling again soon and fear I'll damage them.'

She raised her eyebrows. 'We're not living in the Dark Ages, you know. It is quite safe to send works abroad these days, galleries do it all the time. Send them in an Artpack, for God's sake.'

'I'm afraid it's also a question of money. I know how valuable his works have become, you see, and the path of the itinerant journalist is a costly one . . .'

From *Pussy's Bow*

Time to write was difficult when I wrote my first novel because I was working full-time, but I managed to take a few weeks off as holidays and then worked late at night. Determination was a big factor – to say, All right, if I'm going to do this I'm going to try to make something happen with it. That's a big gamble, especially when, like me, you'd worked in publishing companies for a number of years. I knew how unlikely it was that you would succeed in getting a novel to publication, and then succeed in selling enough to find a niche. To succeed you need a certain dedication and focus, and obviously you need to be able to tell a story.

————

When I'm writing a draft on a computer I'll go through it and through it and through it. I might say each day, I'm going to write new chapters. But then I start reading some of the old ones and I get working on them, so I'm never quite sure how it's going to pan out in terms of the old-fashioned idea of draft. I don't have a draft printed up and then go through it and do another one – it's a constantly changing process as I write. If I get a bit of a block or feel like I can't write new material, it's often easy for me to go through some other chapters and tweak them a bit, then I sometimes find myself ready to write something new.

————

The more you can promote your book, the more likely it is to sell. Books actually don't have a terribly long promotional life. A lot of books can be returned to the publishers after three or four months on the shelves. If you don't get a lot of them sold in those first three months, it's going to be very difficult to do it afterwards, so I always do whatever I can to talk about the books and to read them and to go to various functions. I think it's very important that you promote your books. If you can read well, or if you can perform well, it's a huge advantage.

————

Getting a tag like 'gay writer' is a double-edged sword. Obviously it places me fairly and squarely in the gay market, and, because there are few enough gay novels coming out, ensures that they will be publicised and, hopefully, a large sector of the gay society will read them.

However, I think there's always a tendency to categorise minority groups who are publishing until they've been accepted enough to be slotted into the general Australian literature scene. Then the gayness isn't such an issue. I read quite broadly and I'm more than happy to be titillated by heterosexual erotica, so I think it's a natural progression that more straight readers are going to be able to cope with a bit of gay sexuality in the context of a novel. As a genre, it's something that probably won't always be as narrowly defined as it is.

———

Just keep writing and writing. That's the key. You can be in your twenties and really want to be a writer and it just might not happen until you're in your thirties. I certainly wanted to be writing things in my twenties, but I'm sure that none of what I wrote was good enough. You just have to keep doing it. It's a long process and it's not necessarily going to make you rich. But I think it's definitely worth it.

acknowledgements

The editors would like to thank the following people whose contributions made this project possible: the writers interviewed, for generously giving their time and for offering their insight and wisdom; the Adelaide Festival of Arts and the organisers of Writers' Week, especially Rose Wight, for helping us with access to the event and their guests; Captain J. McGann of the Adelaide Universities Regiment, Australian Army Reserve for allowing us to use the Officers' Mess for interviewing the writers; Deb Kandelaars for typing the transcripts; Josephine Koerner for excellent research and organisation; John Griffin for contributing questions; the publishers for their kind cooperation; and, finally, our families for their support and encouragement.

The following extracts are reproduced with permission: page 5 from *Big Women* by Fay Weldon, HarperCollins, 1998; pages 9–10 from *Darcy's Utopia* by Fay Weldon, HarperCollins, 1990; page 17 from *An Equal Music* by Vikram Seth, Phoenix House, 1999; pages 20–21 from *A Suitable Boy* by Vikram Seth, Phoenix House, 1993; pages 29–30 & 33–34 from *Tin Toys* by

Anson Cameron, Pan Macmillan, 2000; pages 39–40 & 42–43 from *The Shark Net* by Robert Drewe, Penguin Books Australia, 2000; pages 49 & 54 from *The Last Life* by Claire Messud, Pan Macmillan, 1999; page 59 from *Shiver* by Nikki Gemmell, published in 1997, reprinted by permission of Random House Australia; page 62 from *Cleave* by Nikki Gemmell, published in 1998, reprinted by permission of Random House Australia (and by permission of Pan Macmillan in the UK); pages 67–68 & 70 from *The French Mathematician* by Tom Petsinis, Penguin Books Australia, 1997; pages 75 & 83 from *Eight Months on Ghazzah Street* by Hilary Mantel, copyright © Hilary Mantel 1988, by permission of A.M. Heath, Authors' Agents; pages 87–88 & 91–92 from *Out of Ireland* by Christopher Koch, published in 1999, reprinted by permission of Random House Australia; page 97 from *King Hereafter* by Dorothy Dunnett, London, 1982 (page 24), reproduced by permission of Penguin Books Ltd; pages 102–103 from *The Disorderly Knights* by Dorothy Dunnett; Random House Australia, 1997; pages 109–110 from *Greylands* by Isobelle Carmody, Penguin Books Australia, 1997; page 114 from *Scatterlings* by Isobelle Carmody, Penguin Books Australia, 1992; pages 121–122 from *Shadows on our Skin* by Jennifer Johnston, Heinemann, 1988; page 125 from *The Railway Station Man* by Jennifer Johnston, Hodder Headline, 1998; page 129 from *Candy* by Luke Davies, Allen & Unwin, Sydney, 1997; page 133 from *Isabelle the Navigator* by Luke Davies, Allen & Unwin, Sydney, 2000; page 139 & 141 excerpts from *The Dancer Upstairs* © Nicholas Shakespeare, 1995, reproduced by permission of The Harvill Press; pages 151–152 from *A River Town* by Thomas Keneally, published by William Heinemann in 1995, reprinted by permission of Random House Australia; page 154 from *The Great Shame* by Thomas Keneally, published in 1998, reprinted by permission of Random House Australia (and by permission of Hodder and Stoughton in the UK); pages 161 & 165–166 from *Freedom Song* by Amit Chaudhuri, Pan Macmillan, 1999; pages 171–172 & 174 from *Mr Darwin's Shooter* by Roger McDonald, published in 1998, reprinted by permission of Random House Australia; 1998; pages 181–182 from *High Five* by Janet Evanovich, Pan Macmillan, 2000; pages 186–187 from *One for the Money* by Janet Evanovich, © Janet Evanovich 1994, Hamish Hamilton; pages 193–194 & 197–198 from *Hiam* by Eva Sallis, Allen & Unwin, Sydney, 1998; page 201 excerpt from *Independence Day* © Richard Ford, 1995, reproduced by permission of The Harvill Press; pages 206–207 excerpt from *The Sportswriter* ©Richard Ford, 1986, reproduced by permission of The Harvill Press; pages 213–214 & 219 from *Lindbergh* by A. Scott Berg, Penguin Putnam Inc., 1998; pages 225–226 & 230 extracts from *Fall on Your Knees* by Ann-Marie MacDonald, published by Jonathan Cape, 1997, used by permission of The Random House Group Limited; pages 235–236 & 240–241 from *Mr Phillips* by John Lanchester, Faber and Faber, 2000; pages 245–246 from *Quill* by Neal Drinnan, Penguin Books Australia, 2000; page 248 from *Pussy's Bow* by Neal Drinnan, Penguin Books Australia, 1999.

Author photographs appear courtesy of: Fay Weldon (page 6), HarperCollins; Vikram Seth (page 18), Amanda Lane and Allen & Unwin; Anson Cameron (page 28), Sara Mcmillan and Pan Macmillan; Robert Drewe (page 34), Reece Scannell and Penguin Books Australia; Claire Messud (page 46), Host and Pan Macmillan; Nikki Gemmell (page 55), Random House Australia; Tom Petsinis (page 62), the author; Christopher Koch (page 81) Random House Australia; Isobelle Carmody (page 98), George Stawicki and Penguin Books Australia; Jennifer Johnston (page 110), Caroline Forbes and Hodder Headline; Luke Davies (page 121), Allen & Unwin; Nicholas Shakespeare (page 131), HarperCollins; Thomas Keneally (page 137), Random House Australia; Amit Chaudhuri (page 148), Jerry Bauer and Pan Macmillan; Roger McDonald (page 156), Random House Australia; Eva Sallis (page 175), Peter Mathew and Allen & Unwin; Richard Ford (page 188), The Harvill Press; Ann-Marie MacDonald (page 208), Nick Seiflow and Random House UK; Neal Drinnan (page 221), Adam Sutherland photography and Penguin Books Australia.

PENGUIN AUSTRALIAN SUMMER STORIES

Sand between the toes, soft-serve ice-cream, the scent of baby oil, the stillness before a thunderstorm – summer's here.

Twenty-one dazzling stories for summer reading by some of Australia's best-loved writers and hottest new voices, evoking languorous days, restless nights and indelible memories of summers past and present.

Robert Drewe · Andy Quan · Helen Garner · Elliot Perlman Brenda Walker · Tom Petsinis · Peter Goldsworthy · Chris Daffey Lily Brett · Derek Hansen · Rachael Treasure · Nick Earls Kay Donovan · Herb Wharton · Gillian Mears · Mena Abdullah and Ray Mathew · David Campbell · Thea Astley · Tim Winton Dorothy Hewett · Amy Witting

THE PENGUIN CENTURY OF AUSTRALIAN
STORIES
edited by Carmel Bird

This landmark collection brings together the best Australian short stories written in the twentieth century.

From early bush life, through the Depression and the Second World War, to the fast lane of contemporary urban existence, Australian short-story writers have explored and reflected our national identity and experience. *The Penguin Century of Australian Stories* represents, in one volume, our finest writers in all their modes: the lively comic fiction of Henry Lawson and Steele Rudd, the distinctive imaginations of Christina Stead and Patrick White, the experimental style of Peter Carey, and the highly lyrical prose of Brenda Walker and James Bradley.

Selected by Carmel Bird, these stories mirror the concerns of Australia's past and present. *The Penguin Century of Australian Stories* will enlighten and entertain for many years to come.